Hope for a Widow's Heart

Quin Sherrer

Quin Sherrer

Romans 15:13

Bless You!

Authentic

Almost no woman knows how to wade through widowhood. However, Quin Sherrer has created an "Rx for women" who suddenly stand alone—feeling out of place, afraid, angry, insane—and perhaps lustful. Or, they are experiencing a sense of relief, accompanied by quiet guilt. *Hope for a Widow's Heart* is remarkable reading even for the new, fragile widow who finds it difficult to concentrate. The author feeds "healing balm" to her in small bites, with tailor-made scriptures, brief prayers, and short testimonies which are transforming. The sharp pain of aloneness diminishes: As Quin Sherrer gently conveys, "God has a future for you, dear one."

Marion Bond West, Author
Contributing Editor, *Guideposts*

Quin Sherrer is a loyal prayer warrior, wise mentor, and dear friend. She has walked the path of widowhood and left guide-posts for others to follow. Quin selflessly opens her heart and invites the widow in, providing consolation for the pain of separation, discipline for the Christian walk, and freedom to experience the joy of new beginnings. *Hope for a Widow's Heart* walks the reader down many paths that lead to one destination—Jesus Christ, our Blessed Hope. Thank you, Quin.

Diana Hagee, Author and Speaker
Cornerstone Church, San Antonio, TX

I have had the privilege of being Quin's pastor and friend and am happy to endorse her latest book. Filled with life and pulsating with hope, *Hope for a Widow's Heart* will be used by God to heal many. With remarkable poignancy, Quin just makes truth come alive!

Dutch Sheets, Director, Christ for the Nations Institute,
Dallas, TX, Bestselling author of *Intercessory Prayer*

No matter what "stage of widowhood" you are in, this book will benefit you. It has been ten years since I watched my husband die on that mountain in the Philippine jungle, but I found this book full of wise words just for me! You will learn from women who have been there.

Gracia Burnham
Author of the bestseller *In the Presence of My Enemies*

Quin Sherrer is the kind of person with whom others feel comfortable sharing their struggles. A widow herself, she relates her own journey and those of widows young and old, in a wide variety of circumstances, through this hardest of passages. It's all here: the confusion, the near-unbearable pain, the mistakes, but also the hard-won wisdom and surprising renewal. This is that rare book: unflinching about the darkness, but rich in hope.

Elizabeth Sherrill
Author of *The Hiding Place* and *All the Way to Heaven*

No one wants to need this book. Every widow does. True to Quin, she offers us an authentic look at the harsh reality of widowhood with hope, humor, and honor! The life stories shared on these pages will capture your heart while some pages may even become tear-stained. I serve on the pastoral staff of a large evangelical multi-campus church in the Dallas-Ft. Worth Metroplex, and I am glad to say we take the biblical exhortation to minister to widows very seriously, as stated in James 1:27. I am thrilled to have a rich resource like *Hope for a Widow's Heart* to put into widows' hands now.

Mary Jo Pierce, Pastor of Prayer and Intercession
Gateway Church, Southlake, TX

I was raised by a widowed mother, so I can identify with many of the heart-to-heart stories in Quin's devotional book. I've always said, "I learned to trust God from my mother." When Quin and I lived in the same city we met regularly to pray for our families. Now that she has entered a new season, she has written this hope-filled book with appropriate prayers, as well as biblical, practical insights to encourage other widows. I highly recommend *Hope for a Widow's Heart*.

Mrs. Dick (Dee) Eastman
Every Home for Christ, Colorado Springs, CO

Almost every day I visit people who have lost a partner. I know of no greater pain in this life. Sorrow is inevitable, but as Christians we do not have to sorrow without hope. Not only has Quin gone through such a time, but she is a very blessed writer, able to put into simple, practical terms great helps for those experiencing this pain. As a long-term pastor to Quin and LeRoy, and having met with them in a small group once a week for six years, I deeply appreciated their commitment to our Lord Jesus Christ. *Hope for a Widow's Heart* will not only bring you comfort and hope, but is a book you can use to minister to others.

Rev. Peter Lord, Pastor Emeritus,
Park Avenue Baptist Church, Titusville, FL,
Author of *The 2959 Plan: A Guide to Communion with God*

I have read at least twenty of Quin Sherrer's books and have enjoyed her gifts as an instructor at the Center for Biblical Studies in Tallahassee, FL. After reading *Hope for a Widow's Heart*, we scheduled her to teach seminars for widows. Our students anticipate the return of this speaker, writer, and motivator. Her book offers practical advice based on eternal truths for a growing percentage of the population. Those who read it will be blessed.

Jo Anne Arnett, President,
Center for Biblical Studies, Tallahassee, FL

What an amazing God we have! He loves and cares for widows, as Quin's book so richly attests. Having been a widow for more than twenty years, I know that the only path to healing is through the grace and mercy of God. *Hope for a Widow's Heart* points the way with gentleness, insight, and understanding. My husband, Jamie, who was Quin's writing coach, said her talent would one day bless the world. I believe this book will do just that.

Mrs. Jamie (Jackie) Buckingham

Hope for a Widow's Heart
Copyright © 2013
Quin Sherrer
Cover design by Barbara LeVan Fisher

Notice: All names have been changed to protect the privacy of those relating these true stories. Any resemblance to people you know by these names is strictly coincidental. Some locations have been changed also.

Published by Authentic Publishers
188 Front Street, Suite 116-44
Franklin, TN 37064
Authentic Publishers is a division of
Authentic Media, Inc.

Printed in the United States of America

Library of Congress Cataloging-in-Publication Data

Sherrer, Quin
Hope for a Widow's Heart: Encouraging reflections for your journey / Quin Sherrer p. cm.

ISBN 978-1-78078-103-7
978-1-78078-203-4 (e-book)

This book is dedicated to . . .
Tommie Jean Woods,
loving friend and prayer partner,
who was with me when my husband,
LeRoy,
left for heaven.
And who herself departed for
heaven before I finished this book.
I treasure your friendship
and your love for the Lord.

And to . . .
My other faithful prayer partners who
prayed for me while I wrote this book:
Julia, Quinett, Sherry, Dorothea, Betty,
Jane, Martha, JoAnne, Fran, Nancy, Kate,
Mary Jo, Kerry, Margus, Janet, Stacy, Judy, and Nita

And a Big Thank You to . . .
All the widows who shared their stories,
though their names have been changed.

And Special Thanks to . . .
Kyle Duncan, Keith Wall, Sherry and Desiree Anderson

Contents

Part Two: Transitioning From Here to There

Part Three: Dealing with Emotions

Part Four: Embracing a New Season

Foreword

Quin and I go back many years. We've served the Lord together in the ministry of Aglow from Quin's early days as a local officer to each level of leadership in which she has served, including the national leadership for the ministry in the United States. I've had the joy of being the recipient of her caring friendship as we have co-labored together through the years.

A well-loved writer, speaker, and encourager, Quin is a respected woman of God throughout Aglow and the body of Christ. Her prolific pen has produced an impressive body of work, with many bestsellers related to the subject of prayer. Her books have impacted countless lives around the world with their truth and practical applications for everyday living.

The book you are holding sprang from Quin's own transition from wife to widow when her beloved husband, LeRoy, was promoted to glory. She weaves together real-life stories from women who have grappled with an often unwanted and unexpected life experience. And with powerful scriptures from the Word of God, Quin offers help and hope to those on their journey of grief. The devotional format allows you to take bite-sized pieces of inspiration as you navigate this new and unfamiliar territory.

Having experienced widowhood myself several years ago, I can identify with many of the truths in this book. In the first week of my husband's passing, a wise friend counseled me to "grieve forward, not backward." Sound advice, which I took to heart. I believe Quin's book will help you to do just that. You will find encouragement for the days when you feel the weight of grief pressing in, as well as the hope you need that, one day, the transition will be complete and you will live again.

Take Quin's hand as she leads you on this pathway from grief to hope, darkness to light, and sadness to new joy. You will find her a warm and comforting companion on your journey.

Jane Hansen Hoyt
President/CEO, Aglow International, Edmonds, WA

Introduction

A Window into a Widow's Heart

Hope for a Widow's Heart is a devotional book for widows, which lets you see into the windows of many widows' hearts—some young, some middle-aged, some in their golden years.

As a widow, hopefully you will identify with those who share their stories and struggles. Some have recovered from much of their grief. Some have finished wading through piles of paperwork. Some still struggle. A few may still remain angry—at themselves, at God, and even at their deceased spouse: *"How could you leave me in this mess?"* they silently ask.

Hope for a Widow's Heart contains personal testimonies, suggested prayers, and faith-filled scriptures for your journey ahead. In order to protect their privacy and allow for deeper transparency, I have changed the names of the widows featured in this book. Through their true stories, you will discover how the Lord enabled many widows to come through their own "shadow of death" to normalcy again. God wants to do that for you too!

As you read, you may shed a tear, but you will also laugh! "I've been there, and have made some of the same blunders," you can say. Standing at a critical crossroads in their lives, these widows share through encouraging reflections how the Lord ministered help and hope to them during various stages of adjustment:

- Handling grief and saying goodbye (giving yourself time to grieve).
- Adjusting to a life passage (as you transition from here to there).
- Dealing with emotions (loneliness, anger, disappointment, bitterness).
- Embracing a new season (struggles with decisions: finances, housing, relatives).
- Regaining hope (letting the Lord console you; laughing again).
- Resolving issues if there was betrayal in your marriage (forgiving, letting go).
- Agreeing with God's Word (partnering with God and a prayer support team).
- Telling women friends what to do before they become widows.

If you are a friend of a widow, this book will help you understand some of their dilemmas—emotional, physical, spiritual, financial—and give you insights on how to reach out to them. Don't skip Appendix A, which suggests ways to prepare for widowhood.

Our heavenly Father wants to be our husband and guide us through whatever today and tomorrow holds. So let's travel with Him on our new journey and allow Him to put hope into our widow's heart!

Blessings,
Quin Sherrer

Part One

Saying Goodbye

1.

Act Alive

I spread a green blanket over my husband's grave and plopped down on it. Opening my small Bible, I began to read it aloud. I was not here to communicate with my husband—I felt that was wrong—but rather to have a talk with the Lord. To reassure myself of His promises for me, now that He was my husband. To hear His voice speaking about my future.

Christmas, just three days away, would mark my 54th wedding anniversary. This year I was planning no celebration. My husband had gone to heaven a few weeks earlier. Today I made the forty-minute drive to deliver a red poinsettia to the grave in the far eastern corner of the cemetery. Here by my husband were the burial sites of my mother, two aunts, and the uncle who gave me away at my wedding. A police station is next door, separated only by a chain link fence.

The breeze from the Gulf of Mexico, just a block away, almost drowned out my voice as I began to quote Psalm 23: "The Lord is my Shepherd, I shall not want."

Then personalizing Psalm 121, I yelled into the wind, "The Lord is my Keeper. The Lord will protect me from all evil; He will keep my soul; He will guard my going out and my coming in forever." Six times, that psalm repeats keeps or preserves, meaning God is my caregiver—and yours.

As other promises leapt into my heart, I proclaimed them even louder: "The Lord is my Provider. He will meet all my needs, according to His riches in glory . . . The Lord is my Comforter . . . "

For the next thirty minutes, I shouted various Scriptures. Policemen came and went, getting in and out of their patrol cars. I didn't care if they heard me. I decreed comforting psalms, warfare Scriptures, prophetic verses—all the while letting God's precious Word minister to my heart as tears spilled onto my blanket.

The Lord seemed to whisper to me, "What do you see?"

Looking around, I observed acres of gravesites and realized I was alone in the cemetery. Before I could respond to His question, His voice came again.

"Yes, everyone here in this place is dead. You are the only one alive. So get up and act alive!"

His direction startled me. "*Get up and act alive*." Yes, that's what I had come to hear. My watershed moment, my turning-around point, had come to me in a cemetery. I would go home and celebrate my anniversary with some of my children and grandchildren on Christmas Day.

The Lord is indeed my keeper! His keeping power will sustain me. I will act alive. I am alive.

What about you? Can you recall the very moment you decided to go on living? If not yet, stop right now and ask God to speak to you. His Word promises that He still has plans for you—plans for you to prosper, plans to give you a hope and a future (see Jeremiah 29:11).

Scripture

The Lord will keep you from harm—he will watch over your life; the Lord will watch over your coming and going both now and forevermore. (Psalm 121:7, 8 NIV)

Prayer

Heavenly Father, please help me adjust to this life-passage, which I did not choose, but must now walk through. Guide me and don't let me miss Your plan for my life. Now, show me what is it You have for me to do, Lord. Help me! Help me to act alive and be fully alive. Amen.

2.

Widowhood: An Exclusive Club

A letter from a widow friend shortly after my husband died set the tone for me to write this book. She wrote:

> I am absolutely convinced that no other person can ever have a clue as to what you are experiencing in your body, soul, and spirit until they have walked a mile in your shoes. *Until she loses a spouse*. Now you are in an exclusive club to which few of your acquaintances belong. I wouldn't wish such desolation on my worst enemy.
>
> I am glad for the Psalms. They express what we want to say but can't. My counselor said that our tears are groanings of the Spirit in us, praying words we can't formulate; just crying out. The fear is irrational, but, oh, so real. You have post-traumatic stress syndrome—from a battle of dealing with death in the face.
>
> But, thank God, we serve a resurrected Savior who redeems everything the enemy has used to hurt us. He identifies with us, and holds us close. He wipes away our tears. He's always there.

If you have endured the loss of your spouse, you may feel alone. But you aren't. You may think no one can understand the depth of your pain, and it's true that many can't. But again, you are not alone. Many others can sympathize and empathize with your heartache and sorrow.

Widowhood is a club none of us volunteered for or wanted to join. But despite our reluctance and remorse at becoming members of this club, we can be assured that others in this sisterhood stand with us shoulder to shoulder, walk with us hand in hand, and support us heart to heart.

Scripture

Give ear to my words, O Lord, consider my meditation. Give heed to the voice of my cry, my King and my God, for to You I will pray. My voice You shall hear in the morning, O Lord; in the morning I will direct it to You, and I will look up. (Psalm 5:1-3)

Prayer

Lord, today as I began to hum the old hymn, *What a Friend We Have in Jesus*, I felt Your arms about me, comforting me, wiping away my tears. Thank You that You will enfold me in Your arms whenever sorrow tries to overtake me. Thank You, Jesus, my Savior, that You understand because You too knew tears and grief. Amen.

What a Friend We Have in Jesus

Can we find a friend so faithful,
Who will all our sorrows share?
Jesus knows our every weakness—
Take it to the Lord in prayer . . .
In his arms He'll take and shield you,
You will find a solace there. Amen.
–Joseph Scriven (1820-1886)

3.

Give Yourself Time to Grieve

Grief is an emotional phenomenon that affects us all differently. But as you will discover, the process is normal and essential to healing our broken heart. Most of us will go through shock, anger, depression, confusion, guilt, and eventually acceptance; some sooner, some later.

Your friends may not give you enough time to recover. Be sure you allow yourself the time to do so.

"I hope you don't take long to grieve, because you have a lot more to accomplish," one younger woman glibly said to me. I wanted to shout, "Leave me alone!"

A pastor's wife had the nerve to tell me, "I hope you didn't grieve since you know where your husband is—with the Lord." I looked at her and walked away.

In his book, *Don't Take My Grief Away from Me*, Doug Manning says, "The problem is that very few people understand the stages or the symptoms [of grief]. Not understanding often results in their reacting to you with 'you ought not to feel like this' or 'you can't think that way.'"[1]

Grief is a major wound that does not heal overnight. Manning continues: "You must have the time and the crutches until you heal. You will heal in your own way and on your own time-table. To get over grief in a hurry does not mean you are superior. To take a long time does not mean you are weak. Quick recovery does not mean you did not love."[2]

Eight months after I buried my husband, I was sitting in the same church where we held his memorial service. Suddenly I began sobbing my heart out. Deep sobs that hadn't come initially now erupted. I knew it was okay to be experiencing this so much later after his death.

Then the woman sitting next to me nudged me and said, "It's time to stop that crying stuff." I ran from the church and finished crying in the privacy of my car.

The encouraging words from a widow friend a few weeks earlier came rushing back to reinforce me. "Don't forget, the purpose of tears is to cleanse you of your pain. So let the tears roll. Cry when you need to." Then she added: "Say aloud, 'This too shall pass' or 'I am an overcomer and I will survive.'"

A minister said, "Grieving has an expiration date. A time will come when you will cry less and less." He was right. But if you are still at the tender stage, don't let others talk you out of it. The God-given grieving process does not involve bottling it up and stuffing it down. Cry! Just cry! Give yourself the freedom to grieve for as long as you need, in the way that you need.

Scripture

My eyes are dim with grief. I call to you, O Lord, every day; I spread out my hands to you. (Psalm 88:9 NIV*)*

Prayer

Thank You that You see my tears and hear my sobs. Thank You, too, that this is only temporary. The time will come when, instead of grieving, I will laugh again. But in the meantime, I am so glad You who created me understand what I am going through. Thank You for giving me the freedom to feel what I need to feel. Amen.

4. Recovery Is a Process

A letter from a friend says it all today:

> It has been a little over four months since my husband went to his eternal home. I never knew how much losing a life partner would hurt and cause the heart to physically feel like it is torn in two. There are no words to explain the many emotions that have transpired. My husband is everywhere I look, in every sunset I see, at the breaking of dawn, in everything I do, yet nowhere to be found.
>
> One of the most comforting things is reading and rereading the many cards and letters our family received. No, it has not been easy and I am still not all that I would like to be, but I am bringing all my energies to bear on this one thing: "reaching forward to those things which are ahead, and pressing on toward the goal of the prize of the upward call of God in Christ Jesus" (Philippians 3:13-14).

The journey out of grief will not be the same for everyone because different personalities respond in different ways. Some take longer than others to go through this unique valley. One friend said after her husband died of a heart attack, she sometimes felt guilty because a relatively small task took longer than she thought it should to complete, leaving her exhausted but often unable to sleep. Her prayer partner helped her understand that grieving is like work, and she needed to make allowances for fatigue by limiting her commitments.

Her solution for sleeplessness was to meditate on God's many blessings while playing soft instrumental worship music. It helped her focus on the Lord instead of on any problems she had so that she could relax and sleep.[3]

You may want to try this too. I did and it really helped me to go to sleep.

Scripture

Thus my heart was grieved. And I was vexed in my mind . . . You hold me by my right hand. You will guide me with your counsel, and afterward receive me to glory. (Psalm 73:21, 23-24)

Prayer

Father, I acknowledge to You my pain and sadness, but I also trust You for total restoration of my body, soul, and spirit. Thank You for Jesus who carried my grief and sorrows, and for promising to bring joy in the morning. In Jesus' name. Amen.

5.

Letters to God

Imagine being married forty-four years and then experiencing the shock of your husband dying just three weeks and four days after being diagnosed with aggressive spine cancer. This is what happened to Marcy.

Not only that, but Marcy missed his memorial service. She had contracted a contagious intestinal disorder, possibly from staying with him in the hospital constantly. So on the morning of his service, she was admitted to the hospital herself. Thankfully, someone videotaped her husband's service for her.

How did she cope with her grief? She had wonderful memories. A couple of days before he died, she conducted what she called her "litany" by thanking him for all the good times.

"I thanked him for dating me, for wanting to marry me," Marcy recalled. "I thanked him for our wedding and our honeymoon. I thanked him for giving us a daughter three years later and a son fifteen months after that. I thanked him for being an example to our children. I thanked him for praying with me every single night. And on and on I went."

Right before he died, Marcy's husband said something she will always cherish: "Honey, I will be loving you forever."

"And I will forever be loving you," she answered back.

Despite those sweet moments, there were sorrowful ones to follow. "In trying to cope with my grief; at first I couldn't concentrate," Marcy said. "So every morning I went to my computer and wrote a letter to God, using a Scripture passage as a beginning place. I poured out my pain, telling God how I missed my husband, how I longed for him. I believe that was exceedingly helpful in my grieving process. I told my children that I really did not know what this journey of grief was going to be like, but I was going to embrace it because their dad was worthy for me to walk through it."

Marcy waited eight months before she took a grief seminar and was glad to know she was not alone in her numbness, shock, or tears. A year later, she took the grief class a second time, which helped her take even more positive steps forward in the healing process. She shared what she learned from classes, reading books, and her own experience:

> Widows should permit themselves to "grieve well" the first six months when they are experiencing general shock and numbness. But don't expect to go through the entire journey of grieving the first six months. Usually within six to eighteen months (perhaps even twenty-four months) is when you are doing the "work" of grieving. Finally around twenty-four months, you start shifting into recognition that this is reality, life as it is. In that third year, you start allowing God to show you the purposes for your life in the future.

Marcy is the first to acknowledge that these are general guidelines, not rules set in stone.

The grieving process differs for each person.

"Still grieving?" I asked her.

"Not quite as much," Marcy answered. "It has been thirty-one months and four days since he left me, and I still miss him terribly. But I plan to teach grief seminars to help other widows on their new journey. God is the one who sustains me."

May you, dear reader, find the right ways and right people to help you walk through your grief. You may even want to write your own letters to God and pour out your heart. Or read His love letters to you in His Word.

Scripture

[The Lord] heals the brokenhearted and binds up their wounds . . .
The Lord takes pleasure . . . in those who hope in His mercy.
(Psalm 147:3,11)

Father, thank You for the Bible verses that tell me how much You love me and that You will heal my broken heart. Renew my faith in them. Thank You for giving me a steadfast husband for the years I had to share with him. Amen.

6.

Don't Get Stuck

Expressing grief in appropriate ways helps us acknowledge the loss, resolve the pain, and then move forward in trusting God with the future. It is important not to get "stuck" in the grief through denial, depression, or blaming. Even in the midst of grief, we have hope because we have access to the promises of God.

Here's how one woman made her way through the grieving process:

When Renee's husband of three years died of cancer, she cried out, "God, where are You?" For a full year all she felt was grief and emptiness. Then at the urging of some friends, she attended a large revival meeting in another state. As she sat down, she prayed, "Lord, if You don't heal my heart right now, tonight, I might never get healed."

As the congregation began singing, someone passed her a note that read: "As I was standing in line, I noticed you. I believe the Lord gave me this word for you. *He says, 'I see your heart, and I will heal your heart this night.'*"

As the singing continued, Renee felt the Lord's hand on her chest, warm and loving, as though He were caressing her heart.

She was flooded with inner happiness, and suddenly she could not stop smiling. She said the joy of the Lord overwhelmed her and bubbled up within her for many days afterward.

When Renee returned home, she started a ministry for hurting people. She also went on four mission trips and, on one of her trips, she met the man who would become her second husband. God had healed her broken heart and restored joy and purpose to her life.[4]

Scripture

I would have lost heart, unless I had believed that I would see the goodness of the Lord in the land of the living. Wait on the Lord; be of good courage, and He shall strengthen your heart; Wait, I say, on the Lord! (Psalm 27:13-14)

Prayer

Lord, mend my broken heart. Forgive me for blaming You for so many disappointments and heal me of my remaining pain and sadness. Restore my self-worth. I declare in faith that I will overcome my current challenges because You will show me how to make it as a single woman again. I thank You in advance for doing that for me. Amen.

7.

Unwrap Your Grave Clothes

You cry alone behind closed doors so no one can see or hear you. Within the solitude and silence of your heart, you say to yourself, *"I am still grieving after many months of aloneness. Tomorrow I will place flowers on his grave and remember the wonderful times we had together. No one can really understand—no one but Jesus, who cried when His friend died."*

You recall the story from God's Word. Lazarus had been in the tomb four days when Jesus finally made His way to the home of His friends in Bethany. When Lazarus' sister Martha heard He was coming, she went to meet Him.

"Lord, if You had been here, my brother would not have died," Martha said.

Jesus told her, "I am the resurrection and the life. He who believes in Me, though he may die, he shall live. And whoever lives and believes in Me shall never die. Do you believe this?" She answered, "Yes, Lord. I believe that You are the Christ, the Son of God, who is to come into the world" (John 11:21, 25-27).

When they took Jesus to where they had laid Lazarus' body, Jesus wept. Then He ordered the stone in front of the tomb removed as He called out, "Lazarus come forth." Lazarus, still bound hand and foot with wrappings and a cloth over his face, was being restored to life. Turning to the bystanders, Jesus gave them instructions: "Unbind him and let him go" (see John 11). Another translation renders the words "loose him" (NASB).

This Greek word for "loose" is *luo*, meaning to put off, break up, destroy.[5] In other words, to set free.

Those closest to us may want to help unwrap some of the layers of "grave clothes"—or grief—we have around us. They want to loosen what keeps us bound. Yet sometimes it is hard to allow them to do so.

When several close friends came to visit a widow I know, they just sat in the room and let her cry. Without saying anything, they offered the best comfort she could have received. Their silence helped her to allow the Lord Himself to begin to unravel her hurts and heal her broken heart. Though they were quiet, she knew they were praying.

In *Becoming Who You Are*, Dutch Sheets comments on the Scripture passage concerning Lazarus:

> You may think it is too late for your breakthrough, that God simply hasn't and won't come through for you . . . But Jesus has other plans and is waiting with resurrection life to reverse the destructive power that has entombed you. His heart is the same today as it was two thousand years ago, and before He is finished you too will hear the words you've longed to hear: "Come forth."[6]

In so many ways, Jesus came to bring freedom—including freedom from the sorrow that keeps us bound up and weighed down. Allow God's Spirit to comfort and console you. Allow God's people to support and sustain you. In time, you will come forth and experience the freedom Jesus wants for all of His children.

Scripture

When Jesus saw [Mary weeping over her dead brother], and the Jews who had come along with her also weeping, he was deeply moved in spirit and troubled. "Where have you laid him?" he asked. "Come and see, Lord," they replied. Jesus wept. Then the Jews said, "See how he loved him!" (John 11:33-36 NIV)

Prayer

Lord, help me to be open when friends want to walk with me through my journey of grief. Jesus, it comforts me to know that You cried over Your deceased friend. You know what it feels like to lose someone you love. But You also set him free. Thank You that I too will come forth! I believe it and look forward to the freedom You are creating in my life. Amen.

8.

He Is Not Here

When the women came to Jesus' tomb to anoint His body on the Sabbath, an angel greeted them with the news, "He is not here!" He was risen, just as He said. All Christians have that same destination when we have accepted Him as our Savior.

In his book *Heaven*, Randy Alcorn says:

> We on this dying Earth can relax and rejoice for our loved ones who are in the presence of Christ. As the apostle Paul tells us, though we naturally grieve at losing loved ones, we are not "to grieve like the rest of men, who have no hope" (1 Thessalonians 4:13). Our parting is not the end of our relationship, only an interruption. We have not "lost" them, because we know where they are. They are experiencing the joy of Christ's presence in a place so wonderful that Christ called it Paradise. And one day, we're told, in a magnificent reunion, they and we "will be with the Lord forever. Therefore encourage each other with these words" (1Thessalonians 4:17-18).[7]

The phone at my house rang so many times in the weeks following my husband's death—calls for him from salesmen, politicians, polltakers, and other strangers. Finally I came up with a standard reply when they insisted on speaking to him, "Well, you will have to call heaven, because that's where he is."

Aren't we glad that we can look forward to going to heaven someday ourselves when we have made Christ our Lord? Naturally, we still grieve as we miss our husbands, who went to heaven ahead of us. One day we will be reunited in God's presence—and that gives us courage and hope to press on in faith.

Scripture

Jesus said, "Are you asking one another what I meant when I said, 'In a little while you will see me no more, and then after a little while you will see me'? Very truly I tell you, you will weep and mourn while the world rejoices. You will grieve, but your grief will turn to joy."
(John 16:19-20 NIV)

Prayer

Lord Jesus, thank You that You are the Resurrection and the Life. Thank You for paying the ultimate sacrifice on the cross so that I can go to heaven too, and remain with You there. But right now help me face today, here on earth. Dry my tears. Heal my heart. May I look forward to what You have in store for me in my days ahead. Amen.

9.

Having a Talk with God

"Alone. I'm simply alone. What am I going to do with my life now?"

Rebecca asked herself this after her husband died. She felt completely isolated because her Christian support group lived four hours away, in the town where she had once taught school. For years they all met weekly to pray for each other. But now, she felt like she might as well live on a different continent.

"I feel trapped because I can't sell our house in this lousy economy," Rebecca said. "We didn't live here long enough for me to make close friends who could pray me through this season. I miss relationships. But it caused me to press into the Lord even more, to depend on Him."

To help combat her "aloneness," Rebecca got herself a small dog. Then she couldn't stay in bed crying all the time since she had something relying on her. It also meant she was not alone. Best of all, each morning as she walked with her dog, she used it as her own personal time with the Lord, calling it her "prayer walk." At first she had legal issues to settle, including a lawsuit initiated by a stepdaughter, so as she walked she reminded the Lord of all the Scriptures about His promised care for her. Though the lawsuit is behind her, she still quotes Scriptures to

Him every morning as they "talk," and she ends with thanksgiving to Him for being such a loving heavenly Father.

Today let's just take some time to talk to the Lord about our loss. Let Him dry our tears, comfort us, soothe us. Tell God how you feel. Share with Him your needs and desires. Disclose everything that's on your heart and mind. Then listen for His response. This kind of "divine dialogue" opens the door and allows Him to bring the reassurance you so desperately need.

Scripture

He who goes out weeping, carrying seed to sow, will return with songs of joy, carrying sheaves with him. (Psalm 126:6 NIV)

Prayer

Lord, I never thought I'd find myself feeling so alone. What anguish and heartache I feel. Thank You for the man who shared my life. God, I know You understand all I am experiencing in these painful days since his departure. So make Your comfort real to me, especially now. I lean into You. I choose to let You do whatever You need to do to bring me to wholeness. Thank You that I can come to You at anytime and pour out my heart. Amen.

10.

Saying Goodbye

Saying goodbye to your loved one who is about to leave this earth is one of the hardest things a wife will ever do. Each expresses her goodbye in her own personal way, depending on the circumstances and surroundings.

Brenda and her sons and grandchildren gathered around her husband to pray and sing hymns to him during his last hours. She told me her grief was mingled with relief for him, since he had suffered so much for three years.

Two nights before Le Roy left us, my daughters and I sat beside his hospital bed and told him once more what a good husband and father he had been. We held his hand, wiped his brow, and expressed our love. Though he was in a semi-coma, we believe he heard us. We finally told him, "We release you—go be with the Lord. Don't worry about us." Our son and his family had already expressed their deep-set feelings to him earlier while he could still communicate. We had played Christian music and read Scripture aloud as we took turns staying in his room those last three weeks, never leaving him alone.

Sadly, not all families have the opportunity to say good-bye in a way they would like to.

Another friend told me, "Had I known it was going to be my husband's last day on earth, I would not have spent the day in town shopping for Christmas. In the ambulance on the way to the hospital, I realized I was already a widow." But she had to let that regret go.

Lonnie was sitting beside her husband in their living room when he suddenly slumped over. A nurse, she tried everything to revive him. She says she went "crazy" at his death because it was so unexpected, and she did not have the chance for any last-minute goodbyes.

Did she have regrets? Of course. Probably all of us have some. How can you say goodbye now that he is gone? Lonnie writes him letters, expressing her heartfelt emotions, and locks them in a special box. Other widows say they find themselves talking aloud, as though he is in the next room. Some like to say goodbye simply by talking to their friends about their last days together with their husband.

Marie prefers to talk to God about her husband, and she sometimes asks God to relay to her Carl something from her heart. For instance, one day she said, "Dear heavenly Father, please tell my sweetheart how much I appreciate all the effort he spent in landscaping our three acres. I picked flowers from our garden today, and I want him to know how much I appreciate the beauty and joy it brings me."

Perhaps you had a chance to say goodbye in your own special, meaningful way. Perhaps you did not. Remember that harboring regrets does nothing but complicate and prolong the grief process. Remember also that though your husband is gone, you can still say goodbye in a special, meaningful way.

Scripture

Brothers, we do not want you to be ignorant about those who fall asleep, or to grieve like the rest of men, who have no hope. We believe that Jesus died and rose again and so we believe that God will bring with Jesus those who have fallen asleep in him.
(1 Thessalonians 4:13-14 NIV)

Prayer

Lord, today I just want to thank You for hope! Amen.

11.

Experiencing That Glory

After my husband's home going, I reread several books by Catherine Marshall, whose pastor-husband, Peter Marshall, died at forty-six. In *To Live Again* she writes of going into his hospital room after a doctor had called her at home to tell her he died peacefully in his sleep. The night before, an ambulance had taken him there with chest pains:

> I was young, had looked on death only twice before. Yet one glance at the still form on the bed and I knew that the man I loved was not there. But the little hospital room was not empty; I was not alone. For a while there was a transcendent glory. Though I did not understand it then and cannot explain it now, I knew that Peter was near me. And beside him, another Presence, the Lord he had served through long years—years stretching back to boyhood experiences on the moors of Scotland . . . Having actually experienced that glory, I thought at that moment that I would never again doubt the fact of immortality. I was also, minute by minute, learning something else . . . that our God can handle even the worst that can happen to us as finite human beings. Since Christ is beside us, no troubles that

> life can bring need cast us adrift . . . I rose to leave the room. I knew that this would be the last time on this earth I would look on my husband's face . . . So there in the hospital room I said my last *au revoir*.[8]

God can give you creative ways to say goodbye if you still feel the need to do that. Just ask Him. Stories from other women in this book may inspire you. Some wrote their sweetheart letters. Others started journals. Still others simply talked to God out loud: "Be sure my Hubby knows this . . . " Do what feels "right" to you and then have no more regrets.

Scripture

Therefore we also, since we are surrounded by so great a cloud of witnesses, let us lay aside every weight, and the sin which so easily ensnares us, and let us run with endurance the race that is set before us, looking unto Jesus, the author and finisher of our faith, who for the joy that was set before Him endured the cross, despising the shame, and has sat down at the right hand of the throne of God. (Hebrews 12:1-2 KJV)

Prayer

Lord, I thank You for my husband and our life together. While I am still grieving over his absence from my life, I can rejoice that he is in Your presence. Thank You that Christ's death made that possible. Now teach me how to live without him. Help me to regain my focus and direction for what lies ahead. Amen.

12.

Life After Saying a Final Goodbye

When you have lost your loved one from an extended illness or an unexpected death—such as in combat, an auto accident, or a massive heart attack—you can't even describe the devastating impact the trauma evokes in your emotions.

You wonder, *"Will I ever wake from this shocking nightmare?"*

Yes, a time will come when you will be on the pathway to healing, saying your final goodbyes as you piece your life back together. "You have to keep on keeping on," several widows told me. Author Doug Manning put it this way:

> It is always most painful to say good-bye in death. No one can prepare you for this goodbye. No one can lessen the hurt. No one can make you want to. Even in the hurt, goodbye can lead to hello . . . Life is not to end with the death of a loved one. You are to grow. You are never supposed to stop growing . . . You have new experiences ahead of you. You have new worlds to explore, new feelings to feel, new relationships to grow, and in the process, a new you can result.[9]

One widow who had endured goodbyes to three husbands told me, "We have to get to a place of total trust in God because He is the only one who knows our future—the only one! So we say our final goodbye and trust our heavenly Father for our tomorrows."

Her tomorrows include getting more involved in the counseling/prayer team at her local church, especially ministering to new widows. Talking to a few good friends helped her verbalize a final goodbye she wished she had said to her husband before he died of a heart attack. Remember, we are all at different stages in this process so maybe all you can do is keep on keeping on.

Scripture

Now to Him who is able to do exceedingly abundantly above all that we ask or think, according to the power that works in us, to Him be glory in the church by Christ Jesus to all generations, forever and ever. Amen. (Ephesians 3:20-21)

Prayer

Lord, show me how to live again. Right now the pain is still so new, so raw. I have a billion hurts and a thousand questions. Please help me put my life in order. I truly desire to experience a fulfilling life, an abundant life. I need the Holy Spirit's help to accomplish it. Thank You for what You have in store for my future. Protect me physically, mentally, emotionally, and financially. Amen.

13.

Taking Too Much Time to Grieve?

Is there such a thing as taking too long to grieve?

Queen Victoria, beloved English monarch in the nineteenth century, is a possible example. She came to the throne at age eighteen, and two years later married her cousin, Albert, from Germany. While she proposed to him, her Uncle Leopold had a part in arranging the union. She wrote to thank her uncle "for the prospect of great happiness you have contributed to give me, in the person of dear Albert . . . He possesses every quality that could be desired to render me perfectly happy." She was married in white, a tradition that other brides soon adopted.

During their twenty-two years of marriage, they had nine children. Albert became an important political advisor to her. But when he was just forty-two, he was diagnosed with typhoid fever and died. Victoria was devastated. She wore black for the rest of her life. She seldom went to London, rarely made official appearances, and remained fairly secluded in her royal residencies.

When she died in 1901, shortly before her eighty-second birthday, she had been queen for 63 years and seven months.

One of Albert's dressing gowns and a plaster cast of his hand were placed in her casket. She had requested a white funeral instead of black, so she was dressed in white, which included wearing her wedding veil.[10]

Did she really grieve for more than forty years? Yes, she had lost her great love. While some people actually stay in a grieving mode a long time, we don't need to do that. God does have plans for us when we are ready to let Him help us transition to the next stages of our lives—to achieve the abundant life He has in store.

Plenty of people try to hurry the grieving process, and, because of that, their healing is incomplete and insufficient. They have "unfinished business." But on the other extreme are those who go on grieving for so long that their healing, too, is never achieved. Their sorrow is prolonged to the point of being unhealthy and counterproductive.

God does not intend for anyone to be stuck in sorrow and grief forever. Take all the time you need to truly work through your pain—and then move into the new place, and become the new person God desires you to be in the new stage of your life.

Scripture

Now may our Lord Jesus Christ Himself, and our God and Father, who has loved us and given us everlasting consolation and good hope by grace, comfort your hearts and establish you in every good word and work. (2 Thessalonians 2:16-17)

Prayer

Lord, please help me to overcome my tendency to grieve beyond what is healthy for my wellbeing. Thank You. Amen.

14. Tale of Two Widows: One Young, One Older

Since our next section will discuss transitions, let's look at two widows whose lives were intertwined as they experienced transitions—an older woman named Naomi and her daughter-in-law, Ruth.

In the Old Testament book of Ruth, we read that Naomi had gone with her husband, Elimelech, and two sons to the pagan land of Moab, leaving her beloved Bethlehem behind because of severe famine. While there, her husband died as did her two sons, who had married Moabite women. When Naomi learns that the Lord has visited her homeland, and now there is wheat and barley, she decides to return.

Upon reaching Bethlehem she calls herself Mara, meaning "bitterness" because she believes the Almighty has dealt bitterly with her during her ten years of absence. Many grieving people have a sense of misplaced blame—that is, they blame the wrong one. God is a gracious, loving Father who watches over us, as this story illustrates.

Ruth, who insisted on going with her mother-in-law, made a commitment to Naomi: " . . . for where you go, I will go, and where you lodge, I will lodge. Your people shall be my people, and your God, my God" (Ruth 1:16 NASB). She has no idea of the blessing that will come upon her for that solemn statement. Though a foreigner, she is embracing Yahweh, the God of Israel.

Ruth asks Naomi to let her go to the field and glean grain "after him in whose sight I may find favor." Naomi answers her, "Go, my daughter" (see Ruth 2:2). Notice she wants "favor," which comes from Hebrew words that mean: to seek mercy; find kindness; kindness shown to poor and needy; negotiation, often in the context of the strong and the weak.[11]

At times I find myself praying for favor when facing difficult situations. I also pray for someone I can talk with about my circumstances, as Ruth did many times with the older and wiser Naomi.

In those days, farmers were required to leave the corners of their fields to be harvested by the poor and strangers. But this was hard work; gleaners carried heavy loads of grain and grew hot and thirsty. Ruth goes to glean in the field after the reapers. "And she happened to come to the part of the field belonging to Boaz, who was of the family of Elimelech" (Ruth 2:3).

What strikes me here is the phrase "she happened to come . . . " Ruth has gleaned in other fields, but she happens to come to Boaz's field, where she stops and finds favor. This was essential for Ruth—and it is for us. We can happen upon the right people to help us in our circumstances. I pray for this almost daily! Sometimes I have trusted the wrong people, but then I happen to come across the right person I need to help solve a problem.

As the story unfolds, Boaz, the wealthy owner of the field, wants to marry Ruth. But there is a closer relative to Naomi's husband who is eligible to redeem their land, marry Ruth, and thus restore the name of Naomi's dead husband. But when he turns down the offer, Boaz is free to marry the beautiful Ruth and become the kinsman-redeemer himself.

The couple had a son, Obed, who was destined to become the grandfather of King David. In fact, it's likely that as a child David kept watch over his father's sheep in the very field where his great grandmother Ruth used to glean. What a turnabout. Reread the short book of Ruth for yourself. Maybe you will unearth some nuggets as I do every time I reread it. For starters:

- God knows your name.
- God knows your circumstances.
- God knows how to remove obstacles that seem impossible to move.
- God has a solution even if you have to change locations or attitudes to find it.
- God can bring the right people into your life at the right time.
- God has a future for you regardless of how hopeless you feel at the moment.

When Ruth gave birth to a son, the women of the village congratulated Naomi with words of encouragement: "Blessed be the Lord, who has not left you this day without a close relative and may his name be famous in Israel. And may he be to you a restorer of life and a nourisher of your old age, for your daughter-in-law, who loves you is better to you than seven sons, has borne him" (Ruth 4:14-15).

To "restore" means to turn back, return, bring back, reverse, retrieve. Its usual sense is to go back to a point of departure.[12]

Indeed, what a transition Naomi experienced. Once bitter, she was now a joyous woman, helping to nurse her precious grandson, Obed, whose name did become famous, appearing in the genealogy of Jesus Christ.

Naomi was restored and blessed. Her provision was far beyond her hopes or dreams. Our heavenly Father watches over us too. Let's just keep trusting Him!

Scripture

For the Lord your God . . . He administers justice for the fatherless and the widow and loves the stranger, giving him food and clothing. Therefore love the stranger, for you were strangers in the land. (Deuteronomy 10:18)

Prayer

Thank You, Lord, that You show no partiality, that You care for the fatherless and the widow and the stranger. Help me to rely on You as my own Redeemer-Kinsman. Amen.

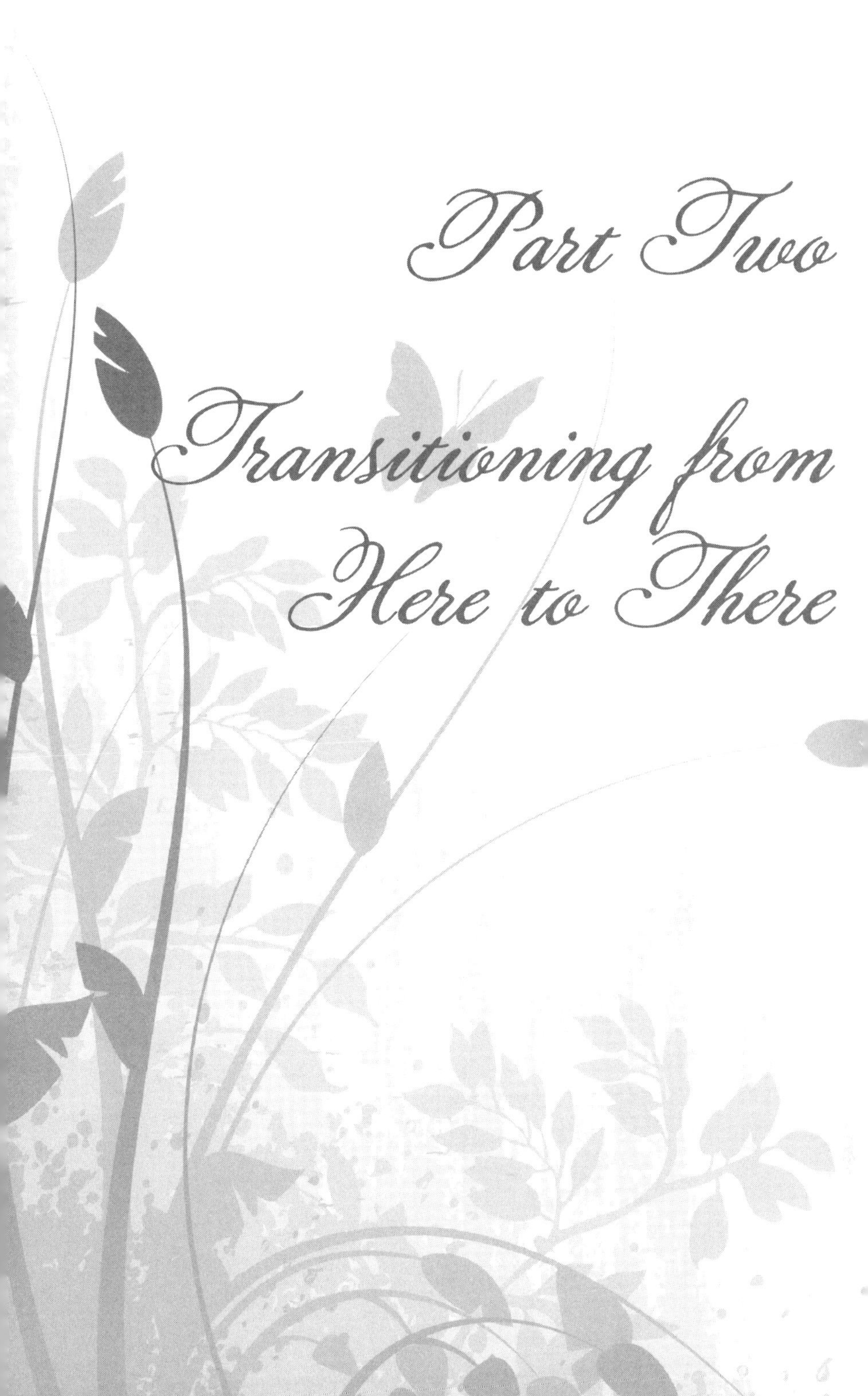

Part Two

Transitioning from Here to There

15.

Dealing with the Aftermath

Transition. That word is sometimes tantalizing and sometimes terrifying, sometimes motivating and sometimes mortifying.

One meaning of transition is to change positions—in our case from wifehood to widowhood. Every year thousands of women must make this adjustment. In the United States, nearly 700,000 women become widows each year and will be widows for an average of fourteen years.[1] In 2009, widows made up 41 percent of all older women, and there were more than four times as many widows (8.9 million) as widowers.[2]

Transition from marriage to singleness can be a scary thing. It requires movement and shifting. It means a whole new life alone, a definite and dramatic change. Let's look at the transitions of three different widows . . .

As Donna's age advanced and her health issues escalated, she agreed with her son that it was time to move to a senior residence where nursing care was available around the clock. She enjoys the amenities: going on field trips in their bus; playing games with other residents; eating meals in the comfortable dining room. She is close enough for family and church friends to visit her, and she is now near a hospital. The downsides: giving up her beautiful home and driving privileges. The reward: her son is largely freed from his full-time responsibility for her care, allowing him to focus more on his career and to visit his adult children in other states more frequently.

Lynda quickly transitioned from her home to a duplex at The Village, a housing complex for retired military widows, where she has much in common with her neighbors. She is glad she can still drive herself to church and shop at the adjoining military base. She recently started a Bible study for widows at the chapel.

Belle, who has a serious medical condition, employs a younger woman to live in her home to cook, clean, and drive her to the clinic for treatments three times a week. Her hired helper lived in the home before her husband died, so she is more like a family member who anticipates Belle's needs. Friends sometimes take Belle for luncheon outings, and she attends church when someone gives her a ride. She is determined to remain in her home as long as she has the finances to afford hired help.

The transition for each of these women has been challenging, and, at times, painful. But each points to God's provision, strength, and support as essential to making the significant adjustments. God's compassion for His children is tender, and He truly wants the best for us. As our loving "Abba"—literally *Daddy*—He is always there to help us through transitions. Our part is to invite Him to walk with us.

You may be in a senior citizen facility, or the home of a relative, or somewhere you did not choose to live. Wherever your "home" is for the present, can you be thankful for it and for those who try to make your life more comfortable?

My paraplegic friend who was in a wheelchair for fifty years used to urge me to enjoy each day as a gift from God—

not even to complain when it rained on my proverbial parade. Great advice, but it was hard for me to apply when I first started plodding my way down the bumpy road of widowhood, especially when some conditions were beyond my control. But I *kept trying and kept trusting*, and it has gotten easier. If you're in the midst of difficult transitions, cling to those words: keep trying and keep trusting. With God's help, you will adjust to your new circumstances.

Scripture

I'm not saying that I have this all together, that I have it made. But I am well on my way, reaching out for Christ, who has so wondrously reached out for me. Friends, don't get me wrong: By no means do I count myself an expert in all of this, but I've got my eye on the goal, where God is beckoning us onward—to Jesus. I'm off and running, and I'm not turning back. (Philippians 3:12-14 THE MESSAGE*)*

Prayer

Lord, thank You for helping me to adjust to living conditions different from what I was accustomed to and different from what I would've chosen. Bless those who minister to me every day, making my life more comfortable. It is my desire not to become a perpetual complainer but to find something positive or joyful each day. Please help me, God. Amen.

16.

How Could He Leave Me in This Mess?

In the last reading, I shared the stories of three women who faced tough transitions. Other widows told me of their challenging circumstances, even while they were able to remain living in their homes. Maybe you can relate to some of these women who found it so hard:

- "Being solely responsible for all bills and finances. Piles of paperwork and decisions loom before you like giants waiting to be slain."
- "Learning to live on less money."
- "Determining what to 'do without' each month to cut expenses."
- "Spending so much time with paperwork, leaving little left for relaxation."
- "Fighting off the fear over my financial status as big expenses accumulated after my husband's death: his hospital and funeral bills; home repairs; insurance costs; credit card charges; taxes; roof replacement; termite riddance; utility bills; my own medical bills; food costs; making business decisions."

- "One enormous plumbing bill cost me bundles when city sewage backed up into our house and leaks damaged all my hardwood floors."
- Dealing with financial "surprises." As one widow described, "My husband had always done the finances, but his disease caused dementia. After his death I opened the checkbook and discovered there was so little left in the account, I nearly fainted. That rocked my world."
- "Learning not all attorneys are your friend. I needed to find ways to shelter and protect my assets, but ended up paying two times what I should have for legal advice. The list goes on of those who take advantage of you—contractors, repairmen, and so on."
- "Having so-called friends become remote, or vanish altogether, since they were used to doing things as couples."
- Sorting through problems when no will or insurance policy was left. As one widow explained, "Since my husband had no will or insurance policy, I had a lot of financial heartaches. We were young and newly married when he died unexpectedly, leaving me with no funds for upcoming expenses. He had not changed his insurance beneficiary from his mom to me. I thought we would live a long time and have plenty of time to make a will."
- Working through feelings of anger or abandonment when your spouse was less than responsible. "I loved my husband deeply," one widow told me, "but I felt violated after his death because he had never told me about his business affairs. I discovered he had run up debt on credit cards he took out in my name, for which I am now responsible for

paying. I didn't even have funds to bury him until I signed over my car title to a relative."

- Paying unexpected and overdue taxes. "I discovered my husband had neglected to pay income taxes for three years," a woman shared with me. "I put all the receipts and paperwork I could find in paper sacks and took them to a friend who was a Certified Public Accountant. He spent hours sorting through it all, and came up with what I owed. I had no clue what to do!"
- Facing possible foreclosure. Here's what one widow told me: "With foreclosure looming on the house a year after my husband's death, I was finally able to sell it for less than half its appraised value. Yet I was glad of getting out of the responsibility of the debt on it as I wanted to move to another state."

Add your own situations and "surprises" to this list. Your "war stories" are probably very painful because they brought you grief and frustration. You are not alone; other women have traveled a similar path. What's more, whatever your unique circumstances, God promises to walk beside you every step of the way. Take your needs, frustrations, and fears to the Lord in prayer. Ask Him to show you a way out of your dilemmas.

Scripture

Plead my cause, O Lord, with those who strive with me; Fight against those who fight against me . . . Vindicate me, O Lord my God, according to Your righteousness. (Psalm 35:1, 24)

Prayer

Thank You, Lord, for rescuing me from situations that seemed so complicated and hopeless. Continue to contend for me! Amen.

17.

Cleaning Up a Money Mess

Financial woes? Money worries? How you long for peace of mind! Nothing slows down a widow's grieving recovery more than anxiety over her financial situation—for the present and for the future. A widow's new income is typically about 63 percent of what she had before her spouse's death.

One woman I spoke with was so taken aback by financial decisions that she did not grieve until eight months after she had buried her husband. She wrote about her frightening financial situation:

> As I faced unchartered waters almost daily, I wanted to ask my husband, "How could you leave me in this mess?" There I was trying to live on half our former income, watching most of my savings slip away, with no unessential spending whatsoever. Our car had to have new tires and major repairs. I had to replace almost all the kitchen appliances because the others broke down. The exterior of the house had to be painted due to mold. I received outrageous medical bills from doctors I never met. My husband had been sick for so long we had neglected many things we should have done.

Many widows discover, with great shock, that their husbands did not plan sufficiently for their future needs, or even basic living expenses. Recently I met with a dozen widows ranging in age from forty-five to eighty-five. None of them felt their husbands had prepared them to manage finances. Most did not even know where to find their documents and records. And some of them had serious financial struggles.

How in the midst of your grief can you get a handle on managing your money? What if financial data is on his computer and you don't even know the password to unlock it? This scenario has happened to far too many widows. You probably need some outside help—a good CPA or a smart son or friend to coach you. Figuring out a budget and sticking to it is a good starting place.

Of course, you and I need God's guidance. Let's ask Him for it daily. You may even feel led to ask for His divine intervention to bring you to a place of prosperity. John wrote, "Beloved, I pray that you may prosper in all things and be in health, just as your soul prospers" (3 John 1:2). He did not hesitate to pray that his friends would "prosper in all things" . . . and neither should we.

Scripture

For wisdom is a defense as money is a defense, but the excellence of knowledge is that wisdom gives life to those who have it.
(Ecclesiastes 7:12)

Prayer

Lord, help me to handle my money challenges with the right attitude. I need wisdom and discernment from You to make wise financial decisions. Help me be a good steward of these resources I have. Lord, I thank You in advance for being available to me, night or day when I cry out for answers. You know my future and I put my trust in You. Amen.

18.

Getting Financially Educated

Widows whose husbands left them with sufficient funds also have difficult decisions to make: stock options, investment opportunities, living on a different budget, deciding whether to move to a smaller place.

"A widow needs to be savvy, street smart, and become financially astute," a woman told me after relating her horror story with a new financial consultant.

Another widow echoed these thoughts when she wrote:

> For ten years I had to deal with incentive stock options that had to be used or lost. The last bunch I just cashed in, built an addition to the house, and gave the children generous amounts at Christmas. I figured I can't take it with me and since they have growing families and college-age kids, they need it now. The key is to find wise counselors, take your time, and pray for wisdom and strength. If you have a good CPA, he is worth his weight in gold. Know your bank and your husband's employers.

Then there's Natalie, whose dilemma is similar to that of many widows. She said:

> After a husband's death, there is an emotional hook that makes dealing with money issues very difficult. After twelve years I still get uptight dealing with finances, and fears creep up. I'm afraid of making a huge mistake in investments, spending unwisely, taking bad advice, or being cheated or scammed. Just being ignorant of the world of money is so scary to a widow. My husband had bonds, which are taxable when I cash them in. That's why I need professionals to help me figure out my taxes. A widow must determine her financial "risk tolerance"—if she is a small, moderate, or large risk taker. I am small. I'd put my money under my mattress if I weren't afraid the house would burn down. I had to educate myself about these matters.

When Natalie was ready to move to a new location not long after her husband's death, she began to pray the prayer that appears below. Use her words as your own prayer or adapt to your unique situation. Tell God what's on your heart. He always has a listening ear.

Scripture

Listen carefully to Me, and eat what is good, And let your soul delight itself in abundance. Incline your ear, and come to Me. (Isaiah 55:2-3)

Prayer

Lord, I need wisdom for handling the finances I have and for investing in the best places. Give me understanding and trustworthy people to be a part of my team. Give me a haven, a place of safety, and a strategic location for my future. I need Your direction! I know I can count on You to provide all I need. Thank You, Lord.

19.

Be Discerning So You Won't Be Deceived

Marilyn and Bud had been married for many years when he was diagnosed with a serious illness. During Bud's last year, Marilyn had been his constant caregiver because he refused to go to a hospital or nursing home. Naturally she was completely exhausted. After his death, she did not slow down because she had to handle his business affairs.

"What people do not realize is how physically and emotionally spent you are after your husband dies," Marilyn said. "I had not slept well in so long that of course I was foggy. When it came time to handle Bud's finances, some of my very close relatives thought I had dementia. They tried to have me declared incompetent. They were after money and would have destroyed my reputation with their vicious lies and rumors. What's really sad is that I had been so kind to them in the past, even giving them money when they needed it."

Thankfully, most family members are genuinely helpful and trustworthy. But widows, especially those still dealing with raw emotions, are vulnerable—and therefore must be vigilant.

Family members weren't the only ones Marilyn had to watch carefully. She also learned to be discerning about attorneys she hired to represent her. When one was overcharging her, she felt the Lord impressed her to "flee" from him.

"I discovered I needed an attorney with drive, one who would fight for me," she added. "If one was not fairly representing me, he had to go. I was not going to let anyone take advantage of me, thinking I was a helpless little widow. I had been a legal secretary and something within me rose up and refused to be intimidated or taken advantage of."

Once, she had the impression that Jesus was standing in front of her by the couch, assuring her He would sustain her no matter who or what came against her. "He never abandoned me," she said. Eventually, she won her case.

The Bible reminds us that God is a "defender" and "champion" of widows (see Psalm 68:5). Maybe no one but the Lord knows the anguish you are going through right now. You may be embroiled in a messy lawsuit. Perhaps relatives have spread hurtful, damaging untruths about you. It could be a relative is trying to wrestle money or property from you. It may be your own child who has turned against you.

Jesus warned his followers to be "wise as serpents and harmless as doves" (Matthew 10:16). Pray that the Lord will help you be discerning, and lean on the trustworthy counselors He has brought into your life.

Scripture

Deliver me, O Lord, from evil men; preserve me from violent men who plan evil in their hearts . . . who have purposed to make my steps stumble. The proud have hidden a snare for me, and cords; they have spread a net by the wayside; they have set traps for me . . . I know that the Lord will maintain the cause of the afflicted and justice for the poor. Surely the righteous shall give thanks to Your name; the upright shall dwell in Your presence. (Psalm 140: 1, 4-5, 12-13)

Prayer

Father, I need advice, so please lead me to dependable, honorable people. I need legal counsel, so please give me discernment about whom to hire to represent me. Thank You for always being there for me when others forsake me. Keep me from being intimidated by those who would try to steal what my husband intended me to have. Thank You for Your loving watchfulness over widows, and that includes me. Amen.

20.

Getting Godly Advice

After her husband of twenty-two years died of cancer, Gloria put herself under the "headship" of her pastor and three other godly men from her church, consulting with them when she faced a dilemma or major decision. Gloria made the final decisions, but she took their advice very seriously. For instance, when a close friend of her husband's wanted to borrow a large sum of money, the advisors told her "No!" At first, she was heartbroken she couldn't help him, but, as it turned out, he proved to be a poor risk.

Gloria married again five years later because she was tired of being single. Her second husband developed health problems, became paralyzed, and could not talk or communicate for six years before he died.

Another five years passed, and Gloria married a friend's brother. On the night of their eleventh anniversary, this man had a stroke and died. "My first husband was the love of my life and we traveled a lot while he was in the military," she said. "My other two husbands were both Christians, but their children didn't get along with me very well."

Since Gloria has had intensive Bible school training, she now hopes to be a volunteer on a church's counseling staff. She feels that the best decision she made was listening to her pastor and the godly men she consulted about major decisions—buying a car, selling a house, making investments, and many others. "The wives of these men were always in agreement that I could consult with them as well," she added.

While Gloria consulted the businessmen from her church during her early years of widowhood, not every widow will find this a feasible solution to her specific situation. Yet God can help you in a way that best meets your needs. Keep searching, keep asking, and keep praying until you find trustworthy advisors. We all need them!

Widowhood is a daunting transition, to be sure, but it isn't the only one we'll face. Others might include: when do we stop driving? do we need to downsize to a smaller place? or which medical treatments should we pursue, if needed? The list goes on and on. I have a friend who displays a plaque that reads, "Lord, Prepare Me for What You Have Prepared for Me." That's a prayer we can all embrace, knowing that one way in which the Lord prepares us is by placing reliable, responsible counselors in our lives.

Scripture

Listen to counsel and receive instruction, that you may be wise in your latter days. There are many plans in a man's heart, nevertheless the Lord's counsel—that will stand. (Proverbs 19:20-21).

Prayer

Lord, You know my complex circumstances and needs even more than I do. Please put on my heart the names of those I can ask for help and prepare them to assist me. Guard me from the wrong ones. Prepare me for what You have prepared for me in my future. I ask in Jesus' name. Amen.

21.

Dealing with Discouragement

Going through another day of discouragement? I know what you mean. I have been there myself . . . many, many times.

We have to make a conscious effort to not allow discouraging thoughts to overwhelm us. King David did this by using "self-talk," which he described this way: "Why are you cast down, O my inner self? And why should you moan over me and be disquieted within me? Hope in God and wait expectantly for Him, for I shall yet praise Him, Who is the help of my countenance, and my God" (Psalm 42:11 AMP).

Sometimes I talk to myself and say, in essence, "Why am I discouraged? If God is for me—and He is—who can be against me?" Then I pray, "God, this is what Your Word says and I am standing on it." Then I will repeat verses I need today, which might be: "Let the weak say, 'I am strong,'" (Joel 3:10); or, "I can do all things through Christ who strengthens me" (Philippians 4:13).

Often I personalize the promises for myself as I read them. A friend sent me a little paperback called *Personal Promise Bible*, which contains just the Psalms and Proverbs with my name actually printed in places throughout those passages that make it very personal to me.[3] I read it every morning. You can do this yourself as you read the Scriptures, by inserting your name in appropriate places.

One widow shared her list of "daily declarations," which she says out loud to help her readjust her attitude and renew her thinking. These phrases help her overcome discouragement; she finds them helpful to repeat:

> I call my life good not bad
> Blessed not distressed
> Peaceful not stormy
> Happy not sad
> Contented not discontented
> Abundant with no lack
> Healthy not sick
> Strong not weak

Still another strategy to overcome discouragement is to replace unhappy memories or thoughts with happy ones. A portion of Paul's letter to the Philippian church as it appears in *The Message* reads like this:

> Summing it all up, friends, I'd say you'll do best by filling your minds and meditating on things true, noble, reputable, authentic, compelling, gracious—the best, not the worst; the beautiful, not the ugly; things to praise, not things to curse. Put into practice what you learned from me, what you heard and saw and realized. Do that, and God, who makes everything work together, will work you into his most excellent harmonies. (Philippians 4:8-9 *The Message*)

May the Lord help you to come to a place where you experience less and less discouragement. May your heart become full of encouragement as your mind is filled with thoughts of God's goodness and blessing.

Scripture

We demolish arguments and every pretension that sets itself up against the knowledge of God, and we take captive every thought to make it obedient to Christ. (2 Corinthians 10:5 NIV)

Prayer

Lord, I want to be free of this discouragement. Help me to concentrate on the beautiful, not the ugly. You have done so many wonderful things for me in the past—I trust You even now for working all things to my benefit. Thank You, thank You. I am so glad to be Your daughter. Amen.

22.

Asking God to Quiet Your Storm

For more than a year I "lived" in Psalm 107. It is about the Hebrew people crying out because of their captivity. But it spoke to me because at least four times, it reads:

> They cried out in their trouble and distress.
> The Lord saved, the Lord delivered.
> Then when they were at their "wits end,"
> He stilled the storm. He hushed the waves.

Their emotions had been as a ship on storm-tossed waters—up to the heavens, then down to the depths of the sea. Their courage had melted away. Can you identify? Haven't you experienced highs and lows since you became a widow? Have you been at your wits' end? I certainly have. Like the Hebrew people, I kept calling out to the Lord for divine intervention and restoration.

Here's the clincher: They did not just cry out for deliverance, but they praised the Lord in the midst of their misery. God brought them to their desired haven.

Maybe you are in need of finding your own desired haven—your own light in your darkness, or peace from the storm.

Maybe you are even anticipating a move to a safe haven. Just as He delivered the Israelites from their bondage, He is ready to do that for you.

We can begin to give thanks to the Lord. Even when we don't feel like it, let's open our mouths and thank Him for His unfailing love and wonderful works. We are assured He hears. He will act.

As I have done so many times, read Psalm 107 for yourself—perhaps over and over—letting the Lord speak to you through some of the verses today.

Scripture

Then they cried to the Lord in their trouble, and he saved them from their distress. He brought them out of darkness and the deepest gloom and broke away their chains. Let them give thanks to the Lord for his unfailing love and his wonderful deeds for men, for he breaks down gates of bronze and cuts through bars of iron. (Psalm 107:13-16 NIV)

Prayer

Lord, I thank You that even in the crises of my life, You can come to calm the storms, hush the seas, deliver and bless me. Thank You that just as You intervened in the lives of the Hebrew people, You will deliver me. Thank You for Your unfailing love toward me. I love You, Lord, and thank You for Your faithfulness. Amen.

23.

Helping Children Cope

A widow with young children has to help them cope with their own grief at a time when she herself is devastated. For Lois's three children, ages twelve, fifteen, and seventeen, it meant their dad, Dan, would not be there to see the oldest graduate in a few months, or build a Christmas manger with his daughter, or coach any of their sports teams.

After Dan learned he had congestive heart failure, not bronchitis as a doctor originally diagnosed, he lived only twenty-one more days. Shock and numbness overwhelmed Lois and the kids. Dan was a businessman, but because he had been a worship leader in their church for sixteen years, music was a big part of their life. And music would play a significant role in the family's healing process.

The evening after Dan's death, Lois gathered the children onto her bed and sang them a song they had heard every night since the day they were born, "Tell Me the Story of Jesus," written by the blind hymn writer Fanny Crosby.

"When we had our first baby, we chose a song we could sing to our children so that even after we had taken our last breath, they would be comforted," Lois said. "That night, I sang it to them just as their dad had every night."

The lyrics include these lines:

Tell me the story of Jesus,
Write on my heart every word;
Tell me the story most precious,
Sweetest that ever was heard.
Tell how the angels in chorus,
Sang as they welcomed His birth,
"Glory to God in the highest!
Peace and good tidings to earth."[4]

Lois also reminded her kids of their family's life verse that she and Dan had adopted when they married: "'For I know the plans that I have for you,' declares the Lord, 'plans for welfare and not for calamity to give you a future and a hope'" (Jeremiah 29:11 NASB).

Lois observed how anger gradually overwhelmed her oldest son, Bart. He was mad at God because He didn't stop his dad from dying. He was restless, giving in to despair. Lois's strategy was to talk to Bart about his dad—a lot.

"Remember the talks you and your dad had about your future, your musical talents?" she said to him. "Bart, what your dad planted inside you came from his heart, and that came from the heart of God. He told you how kind and compassionate you are and how proud he was of you. Your future is not going to change just because your dad is not here. Your dad's reflection will always be in your heart. He wanted you to go on with your music because he believed in your talent. That goes for me too—I believe in you."

Lois had many conversations with him over the next three years to get him to see God's plan for his life, even with his dad gone. She'd remind him who he was in Christ. Because his dad had carefully planned for his family's financial future, Bart was able to leave that fall for college, where he excelled as a percussionist with the orchestra.

The second son, Carl, experienced grief differently. He too was interested in music, playing guitar and piano, so Lois gave him some of his dad's handwritten songs. She told him that many of the all-time greatest songs were written out of sorrow and hurt; she encouraged him to express his feelings through songs. She mentioned that the hymn "It Is Well with My Soul" was written after Horatio Spafford's four daughters drowned when the ship they were aboard sank in the Atlantic. So Carl began to write his own songs and even got one published. Today, he teaches music classes to high school students while he completes his college education.

Rhonda, the youngest, had never shown any musical ability, but Lois had secretly hoped she could learn to play the piano. One day a couple in their church gave the family a beautiful piano. Rhonda sat down and played a song she had recently heard, just by ear. "Music was the outlet for my children's healing," Lois explained, "because that was the heart of their dad."

To handle her own grief, Lois curled up at night in a recliner after she had the kids tucked in and envisioned herself sitting in the lap of God. "Lord, just let me sit here with You holding me," she'd say amid sobs. "Don't let me go." She read the Word of God even when she didn't feel like it, finding that the Lord spoke to her and brought healing.

What's more, her grieving was made easier by happy memories. A day before her husband died, he sang "My Only Love" to her from his hospital bed—the same song he had sung at their wedding.

On her twentieth anniversary, a friend came over to help her sort through cards and papers she had not tackled since Dan's death over a year earlier. They discovered a card he had given her on their tenth anniversary on which he had written, "I will love you just as much on our twentieth as I do on our tenth." She felt it was his gift to her; more happy memories. She was transitioning well, without even realizing it.

Scripture

Have I not commanded you? Be strong and of good courage; do not be afraid, nor be dismayed, for the Lord your God is with you wherever you go. (Joshua 1:9)

Prayer

Thank You, Lord, for the comforting hymn by Fanny Crosby. I echo the lyrics and join in saying, "Glory to God in the highest!" Thank You for moving me toward healing. Thank You for being my heart's hope!

24.

Considering Your Children's Pain

Corine wished she had been more considerate of her children when her husband died suddenly of a heart attack while in his early fifties. She wrote about it:

> After the death of a spouse, at first you have a sense of isolation, like you are marooned on an island with no one to help. That was my predicament. The agony of aloneness was so wrenching to me at first—and the crying so wearying—that I was desperate to move beyond it.
>
> I wasn't thinking about my adult kids at all. I felt so alone as if they were not in the picture. I just didn't think of them when it came time to clean out my husband's stuff, like tools or clothes. I did it all alone or with one friend who came over. That was dumb. I sold some of my husband's coins to a dealer; now I know that our oldest would have liked them. But it's too late.
>
> I finally had a long talk and cry around the kitchen table with my four grown children. I told them how selfish I had been by not thinking of them or their grief. Their process was different from my own, so I didn't identify with them.

My advice now is to go slowly with decisions. Give yourself time to grasp what you are doing, not just for yourself, but also, your family. While grieving, everyone is so raw. We do thoughtless things, and make hasty decisions. A lot of it is out of fear. I just wanted to move on, as fast as possible. For me it was like a time of temporary insanity, for sure.

Just a year before Duane died, we sold the home we had lived in for most of our married life because he wanted to move. But the new house was definitely not home to the kids or me. So in this instance I did not go slowly with a decision.

Thankfully, the Lord eventually orchestrated circumstances so we could move back to our old neighborhood, just two doors down from our former home, close to relatives and caring people. I felt so comforted in the neighborhood. It was such an amazing time, seeing God step in and arrange things.

God does so much for me, even redeeming my mistakes. Today the children and I talk openly about most anything. I don't try to hide my feelings anymore, nor do they. Even if it hurts for the moment, we say what is on our hearts, clear the air, hug, and go on living. That's what my husband would want us to do.

Do you and your children have issues that need to be talked through? Maybe some forgiveness that needs to be extended? Any conflicts that need to be resolved? If so, ask the Lord where to start and how to do it. Don't give up if it doesn't happen immediately. Trust Him to open the way and be ready when the opportunity is ripe.

Scripture

Pure and undefiled religion before God and the Father is this: to visit orphans and widows in their trouble, and to keep oneself unspotted from the world. (James 1:27)

Prayer

Thank You, my Father, for watching over me. Thank You for redeeming some of the early mistakes I made with my children when my husband died—hasty, thoughtless actions. Keep me on the right track so I won't stumble again. Help me keep my relationship with them open, honest, understanding, and loving. You know how I love them, so show me ways to let them know too. Thank You for knowing my thoughts and the intents of my heart. Help me keep them pure. Amen.

25.

Removing "Stuff," Moving On

It is a big step, sometimes a heartrending step, to clear out your husband's belongings—clothes, tools, fishing gear, coins, cards and letters, old tax records, and boxes of who-knows-what-else. What to keep? What to toss? What is important? What is of sentimental value? Some women get rid of stuff too soon. Some postpone the ordeal for many months.

Rhonda waited three years to even look inside her husband's bedside table drawers because they contained his most personal belongings: his Bible, diary, and letters. She was so relieved and proud of herself the day she finally got that job behind her.

Sometimes you may feel the need to get rid of things related to your husband's death, though not necessarily his personal belongings. Cindy sent me this page from her journal on the day she finally decided to burn some pages she'd written:

> As I journey back to the months following Donald's death, I am ready to put it all behind me. But as I see little notes that brought life and hope to me then, I hate to burn them. That is my first impulse, though: Destroy them. Some things I don't

want others to read. Why are we ashamed of our weaknesses? The fallen nature likes darkness, I guess. So we want to hide or delete the uglier stuff, or at least I do.

I need to discern what I've written that would be helpful for others (my kids) and therefore kept, and what would be demoralizing and therefore discarded. I pray I will know what to keep and what to throw away.

It is finally a wonderfully warm day and the birds are loudly announcing their return. I'm doing a little spring cleaning and it feels so freeing to burn some stuff from the past! I love a day like this—fresh and liberating.

Have you yet come to a day that is fresh and spring-like? Maybe you did some housecleaning. Maybe you finally cleared the garage of your husband's tools, or emptied the closet of his clothes, or even discarded the clutter from his office file drawers. Maybe some cobwebs in your mind got swept away too. Thank God today for that—whatever you were able to "put behind" you.

Dear one, listen up. It is perfectly okay if you haven't reached this major milestone yet. Just wait! You will eventually. But in the meantime, look forward to the spring, when your cold winter season is past. Rejoice! Listen for the birdsong.

Scripture

For lo, the winter is past, the rain is over and gone. The flowers appear on the earth, the time of singing has come, and the voice of the turtle-dove is heard in our land. The fig tree puts forth her green figs and the vines with the tender grapes give a good smell. Rise up, my love, my fair one, and come away! (Song of Solomon 2:11-13)

Prayer

Father, as You heal my heart of disappointment, sadness, and pain, help me to know when it is time to clear out things that keep me anchored to the past in an unhealthy way. Guide me so I'll know the memory-laden items to keep and treasure, as well as the ones I need to discard for the sake of healing and freedom. Thank You that springtime always follows winter. Father, let me experience spring, with all its warmth and renewal. Amen.

26.

Restore All

Maybe you have read the story in the Old Testament of the Shunammite woman, who built an upper room on her home for the prophet Elisha to stay in when he came to her community. He was so touched by her kindness that he wanted to do something special for her. Hers is an incredible story of God's intervention.

When Elisha learns that the Shunammite woman and her older husband have no children, he prophesies that in the spring she will have a son—which she does. We can only imagine her joy in becoming a mother, a dream of every Israelite wife. But some time later, during the harvest season, her son dies. She lays his lifeless body on Elisha's bed, shuts the door, and goes to find the prophet. On the way, Elisha's servant Gehazi inquires about the child. The woman's faith is so strong that she answers, "It is well."

She reaches Elisha, tells him about her son, and asks him to intervene. Elisha hurries to his room and stretches himself upon the child until his flesh is warm. When the lad sneezes and opens his eyes, the prophet calls the mother to come and find her son completely restored (see 2 Kings 4:36).

Later, when a famine plagues Shunem, this woman has become a widow. Elisha, God's spokesman in her life, tells her to take her son and go to the land of the Philistines until the famine is over. She obeys. Seven years later, she returns to her home, only to find that her house and land have been confiscated.

What can she do? She decides to go directly to King Jehoram to appeal for the return of her possessions. When she gets there, God has already sent an advocate to present her case. Gehazi, servant of Elisha, is at that moment talking to the king about her. When Gehazi notices her standing there, he tells the king that she is the woman whose son Elisha restored to life (see 2 Kings 8:1-5).

She acknowledges the truth. The king tells one of his officers to "restore all that was hers and all the produce of the field from the day that she left the land even until now" (2 Kings 8:6 NASB).

Seven years of living among the heathen Philistines, then to come home to find what you left behind is not yours . . . what a blow! But the king, the one in authority over all the land, commands that her possessions be restored and even profits from the produce of the field repaid. Talk about favor for a widow! That's restoration.

Jesus is our Advocate and King, so we go to Him with our problems, standing on His promises to us. His promises are "yes" and "amen" (see 2 Corinthians 1:20).

There will be times when you, as a widow, yearn for a touch from the Lord—for Him to restore, renew, reinvigorate, or revive you. You may even long for Him to repay something that was stolen. I discovered sixty-one references to *restore* in the NIV Bible translation. Some included promises to various people that the Lord will: Restore life, land, fortunes, structures, health, joy. He will restore one to his rightful place, repair the broken places, and restore its ruins. He said He Himself will restore you and make you strong, firm, and steadfast.

Do you need restoration in some aspect of your life? Come before the King, knowing that He is always fair, generous, and just. Wait upon Him, believing that He will respond to your pleas with grace and loving-kindness.

Scripture

I'll refresh tired bodies; I'll restore tired souls. Just then I woke up and looked around—what a pleasant and satisfying sleep!
(Jeremiah 31:25-26 THE MESSAGE*)*

Prayer

Lord, thank You for examples in Your Word of Your desire to restore. You did miracles for the Shunammite widow, and You can do miracles for me. I present my situation to You and ask You to intervene, restoring to me what I have lost (name the problem or dilemma). You are truly the Restorer of broken hearts and broken dreams. Lord, thank You that I am becoming refreshed and beginning to be restored through Your power. Amen.

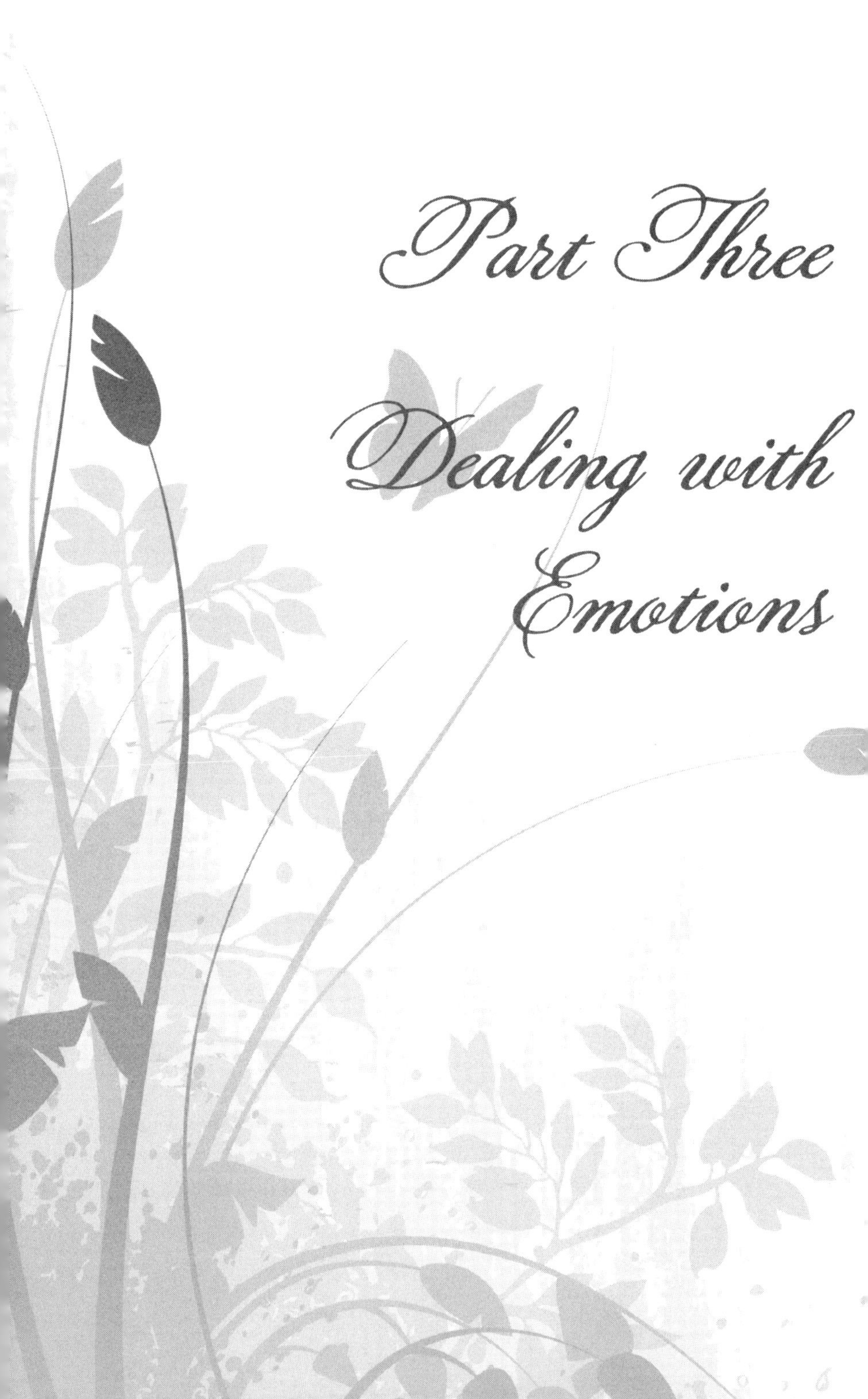

Part Three

Dealing with Emotions

27.

Confronting Anger

We all have them—those "uglies" in our life we wish we didn't have and hate to admit we do. We can identify with the apostle Paul when he said, "For what I want to do I do not do, but what I hate I do" (Romans 7:15 NIV). Strong emotions can almost immobilize us if we let them have free rein: fear, worry, anger, guilt, or unforgiveness. Are they magnified after we go through the trauma of losing a spouse? I've often wondered.

The truth is that if your loved one had a lingering illness and you were the prime caregiver, you probably put your own feelings, needs, or even health issues on hold until "later" . . . and when later came, the impact hit you broadside. Suddenly you must deal with emotions you never expected. This can happen to a widow no matter what her circumstances.

Did you lose your temper more often after your Honey died? Anger took me by surprise. I didn't know I had so much hostility and fury in me until I was constantly harassed after his death by the unexpected bumps in my road. Author Genevieve Ginsburg explains:

> Widows are angry. Some admit it, some deny it, and some don't even know it. They differ only in where and how they focus that anger. Unvented wrath has to go someplace . . . your internalized anger will surely come out via one outlet or another: guilt, depression, self-recrimination, or sugar-coated bitterness.[1]

Ginsburg further says anger is a state of grief, suggesting that you may even be angry with your dead husband: "You had no right to leave me in such a mess."[2] At first for me, I got mad at other people, not so much at my husband. Often my behavior was horrid.

I exploded at a bank manager because their corporate office canceled my credit card without notifying me. Several friends warned me this had happened to them, but I dismissed the thought until a collection agency called, insisting I owed money even though I didn't. The bank manager listened to me vent, and then ordered another credit card in my name.

"I'm no dummy," I told her. "I can handle money."

"Of course you can," she said, smiling.

A widow named Kathy told me that after her husband died, one of her close friends said, "I know how you feel because I just lost my dog." Kathy was mad, just crushed. But sometime later, that friend's fifty-one-year-old sister died of cancer, and she experienced the heartbreak of losing a loved one. She regretted her earlier remark to Kathy, and in fact, she apologized for it.

Someone once said, "It is far easier for me to react in my pain than to respond in love when someone hurts me or acts unjustly."

I don't know about you but for a few months after my husband's death, I experienced a hurricane of misspent anger. I truly needed to forgive myself for my ranting, illogical thinking, and ungodly behavior. And I needed the Lord to forgive me for the way I reacted toward some people.

If you have had such experiences—reacting out of your pain rather than responding in love to injustice—you may want to ask God to forgive you too. Then forgive yourself. After all, your behavior is not unusual for a grieving widow. Emotions are God-given and expressing them in healthy ways is God's best for us. But when they control us, we need His help to overcome any attitude or action that is wrong.

Scripture

But the fruit of the Spirit is love, joy, peace, patience, kindness, goodness, faithfulness, gentleness and self-control . . . Since we live by the Spirit, let us keep in step with the Spirit.
(Galatians 5:22, 25 NIV)

Prayer

Lord, please forgive me for losing my temper; help me to get it under control. I declare that I will not be driven by anger, but by the Holy Spirit. I ask You, Lord, to release the fruit of the Spirit into my soul—mind, will, and emotions—for I truly want to exhibit this fruit in my life. I claim John 8:36: "Therefore if the Son makes you free, you shall be free indeed." Amen.

28.

"I Need a Scream Room"

Go on—admit it. You're struggling with anger, aren't you? That's a safe assumption, since most widows experience some residual resentment, if not rage. Maybe you can relate to what these widows said about their struggles with anger:

> I have so much internalized anger that I'm like a pressure cooker ready to blow—and I do sometimes. Almost immediately, I am ashamed that I vented at the stranger who called about the need for me to sign yet another paper. Or at the doctor who never even saw my husband, but put the wrong reason for his death. I had to pay more money for new death certificates after I finally found a doctor who would look at my husband's medical records and change that wrong reason for his death.

> I am angry about an outrageous bill from a doctor I never knew treated him. And at the company who canceled insurance on our home. And it goes on and on. I need a scream room! How much more can I take? My blood pressure is sky high.

> I really struggled with the relatives who tried to tell me how to run my affairs. My husband's sister tried to micromanage our lives when my husband was in the hospital, and after his death. She continued badgering me as I tried to settle up his estate. I decided not to let her guilt trips intimidate me, and I finally severed our relationship. It was just too stressful for me to be around her.

> I get very upset with all the people I have to deal with who just do not understand what a fragile widow I am right now. Lord, I cry for mercy!

When memories of your "tempter tantrums" flash across your mind, ask the Lord to forgive you and erase them completely from your mind. Then tell Him that you receive His forgiveness. You can do so with assurance, echoing the psalmist's words, "As far as the east is from the west, so far has He removed our transgressions from us. As a father pities his children, so the Lord pities those who fear Him" (Psalm 103:12-13).

Scripture

In your anger do not sin: do not let the sun go down while you are still angry, and do not give the devil a foothold . . . Get rid of all bitterness, rage and anger, brawling and slander, along with every form of malice. Be kind and compassionate to one another, forgiving each other just as in Christ God forgave you. (Ephesians 4:26-27, 31-32 NIV)

Prayer

Heavenly Father, forgive me for expressing my feelings of anger, bitterness, and resentment in harmful, hurtful ways. I was deeply wounded and angry at what [name the person] said/did. But now I choose to forgive [name] for what was done. And I ask that You would forgive me for acting so unlike You, for losing my cool and snapping. Lord, please help me change my wrong behavior. Even as I ask You to forgive me, I receive Your loving forgiveness. In Jesus' name. Amen.

29.

Extending Forgiveness

During our transition into widowhood, there will be plenty of people we will need to forgive.

Who are they? Your spouse? Child? Stepchild? Relative? Friend? Doctor? Hospital billing service?

Maybe God.

Maybe yourself.

Often we need to first own up to our unforgiveness, and then forgive, so God can set us free. Oh, I will not say it is easy! It's one of the hardest things we will do.

What does it mean to forgive? Whether you are looking for definitions in the dictionary or the Bible, you can find several meanings:

- to absolve from payment (to cancel a debt)
- to excuse from a fault or an offense
- to renounce anger or resentment against
- to bestow a favor unconditionally
- to release, set at liberty, unchain[3]

Forgiveness, as you have probably discovered, is often a process. I heard the Dutch evangelist Corrie ten Boom share an illustration some years ago that helped me in this area. Following her release from a Nazi concentration camp, Corrie was speaking in Europe when a young woman asked her to pray with her. Corrie directed her attention to the church bell, as she said:

> Up in that church tower is a bell which is rung by pulling a rope. After the sexton lets go of the rope, the bell keeps on swinging. First ding, then dong. Slower and slower until there is a final dong and it stops. When we forgive someone, we take our hands off the rope. But if we have been tugging at the grievances for a long time, we must not be surprised when the old angry thoughts keep coming for a while. They are just the ding-dongs of the old bell slowing down.[4]

Here are some suggested steps to help you through the process:

1. Acknowledge the wounding you suffered because of the person's actions toward you. Tell the Lord exactly how you feel.
2. Choose to forgive; this is an act of your will—a decision, not an emotion.
3. Recognize that this person had a great need in her life when she hurt you. Use Jesus' prayer in Luke 23:34 as a model.
4. Pray for the person; bless, don't curse (see Luke 6:28, 35).
5. Ask God to forgive you for the anger and resentment you have against the person who offended you—or against

God Himself, if you have blamed Him for allowing the offense to happen.

6. Accept God's forgiveness. Actually say something like, "I receive Your forgiveness. Thank You for freeing me from the bondage of unforgiveness."
7. Take care in how you talk about what happened to hurt you. As one pastor said, "Stop nursing and rehearsing your hurts."[5]

Forgiveness is usually not a one-time act. We will have all kinds of memories or flashbacks that we need to ask Christ to take away as we choose to forgive. For me, it was to forgive the following people: myself, for some of the choices I made in caring for my husband; the doctor who missed the diagnosis; and the hospital's financial officer who kept billing me without cause.

When we forgive, we release the offending person from our own judgment, surrendering it to God to judge him or her.[6] Paul wrote: "But one whom you forgive anything, I forgive also; for indeed what I have forgiven, if I have forgiven anything, I did it for your sakes in the presence of Christ, in order that no advantage would be taken of us by Satan, for we are not ignorant of his schemes" (2 Corinthians 2:10-11 NASB). It sounds as though Paul is saying unforgiveness is one of Satan's schemes.

You may want to make a list and, one by one, go through the act of forgiving. But as Corrie ten Boom said, it may take a while before the final gong sounds and you realize you have finally released that person or situation. Then you'll realize you are no longer chained to that individual or the harmful act. You are free!

Scripture

And whenever you stand praying, if you have anything against anyone, forgive him, that your Father in heaven may also forgive you your trespasses. But if you do not forgive, neither will your Father in heaven forgive your trespasses. (Mark 11:25-26)

Prayer

Lord, because I want You to forgive me, I choose to forgive those who have wounded me (name them). Thank You for helping me work my way through the process and for giving me mercy. Please help me show mercy to others. Amen.

30.

Facing Fear

Fear and worry are among the ugliest apprehensions we widows have to overcome when we suddenly face life alone. Fear of the future. Fear of failure. Fear of financial loss. Fear that you will make wrong decisions. Fear of losing friends. Fear of never being loved. Fear of being ignored, rejected, or abandoned. Fear of losing another relationship or loved one. Even fear of death.

Fear can give us stress, rob us of sleep, and can even bring on high blood pressure, and other health-related problems.

One young woman woke up one morning just a few months after her wedding to find her husband dead beside her. In addition to her shock and sorrow, she faced an uncertain future with no insurance. She wrote about her early fears:

> I ended up moving back in with my parents. Financially I could not afford our apartment after my husband died, and I had a fear of living alone. I have had to deal with fear of moving on, fear of the future, and fear of making mistakes regarding my future. I have lots more worry now than when I was married because when the worst happens, you worry about the worst happening again. Because of the fear of a future spouse dying or

> something awful happening, I have wondered if I even want to get married again. And someone who has not been through it usually gives you a pat answer, like, "Oh, that won't happen," or, "Everybody dies sometime."
>
> You have to get honest with God and ask Him to heal your heart and re-establish your belief in His goodness. I started doing that by reading my Bible and memorizing Scriptures that give me hope. I also write my thoughts in a journal. God does have good plans for me. He is seeing me through the "valley of the shadow of death," and it is good to be able to move through it all at my own pace.

Our antidote for fear is simple faith and trust in God, as this young widow was learning. Use some of her strategies, mix in some of your own, and allow the Lord to work in your heart. Fear may be part of the human condition, but we have a heaven-sent Spirit to give us power, strength, and courage.

So do not fear, for I am with you; do not be dismayed, for I am your God. I will strengthen you and help you; I will uphold you with my righteous right hand. (Isaiah 41:10 NIV)

Prayer

Please forgive me for having a bundle of irrational fears. I truly want to have faith for my future. Help me change my thought patterns—my "stinking thinking"—because I know Your Word says that as a person thinks so is she. I want to keep my mind focused on You so I don't entertain thoughts that cause me to lose peace, but instead show that my trust is in God. Amen.

31.

Fear vs. Faith

When we acknowledge our specific fears, we have started on the road to overcoming them. God can now begin to show us ways to confront our fear-producing situations. Throughout the Bible, we read verses that assure us our God is there, watching over us. One of my favorites was when David said of God:

> You are my hiding place; You shall preserve me from trouble; You shall surround me with songs of deliverance. I [God] will instruct you and teach you in the way you should go; I will guide you with My eye (Psalm 32:7-8).

Another psalm is often encouraging to those fearful of living alone, since it speaks of safety and the abiding presence of God. Parts of it read:

> You shall not be afraid of the terror by night, nor of the arrow that flies by day, nor of the pestilence that walks in darkness, nor of the destruction that lays waste at noonday . . . Because you have made the LORD, who is my refuge, even the Most High, your dwelling place, no evil shall befall you, nor shall any plague come near your

> dwelling; for He shall give His angels charge over you, to keep you in all your ways (Psalm 91:5-6, 9-11).

A wise woman once told me: "Fear and faith both start out on the same path, because both believe something is going to happen. Fear anticipates something bad; faith anticipates something good. Fear is the opposite of faith. You can choose faith that God will help you through your ordeal, or you can let fear devour you. So why not place your faith in God with trust, confidence, and assurance that He is working for your best?"

When we are afraid, God wants us to cry out to Him. He told us through Jeremiah: "Call to Me and I will answer you and show you great and mighty things, fenced in and hidden, which you do not know—do not distinguish and recognize, have knowledge of and understand" (Jeremiah 33:3 AMP).

Scripture

Now faith is the substance of things hoped for, the evidence of things not seen. . . Without faith it is impossible to please Him, for he who comes to God must believe that He is, and that He is a rewarder of those who diligently seek Him. (Hebrews 11:1, 6)

Prayer

Lord, show me things I need to know. Help me become an overcomer and the fearless woman You created me to be. I ask this in the name of Jesus Christ of Nazareth, my loving Savior. Amen.

32.

The beloved Quaker author Hannah Whitall Smith penned something many years ago that speaks to my heart:

> Our lives are full of supposes. Suppose this should happen, or suppose that should happen; what could we do; how could we bear it? But, if we are living in the "high tower" of the dwelling place of God, all these supposes will drop out of our lives . . . Even when walking through the valley of death, the psalmist could say, "I will fear no evil"; and if we are dwelling in God, we can say so too.[7]

Lena embraced fear like a garment, especially after she learned her husband of thirty-three years had cancer in his lymph nodes. Fear overwhelmed her when doctors pronounced his death sentence. How would she make it? The morning after she received the devastating news, she drove in the pouring rain fifty miles to the hospital. Tears blurred her eyes so badly she could hardly see the road.

The words *praise Him* came to her thoughts. She didn't feel like praising God, but what else did she have to do for the next hour, besides cry? Between sobs she would say, "Praise the Lord. I love You, Lord. I trust You, Lord. Great is the Lord and greatly to be praised." She continued saying short praises but could not form long ones.

Later, as she walked into the hospital lobby, she felt something like a heavy winter coat slip from her shoulders. She knew the weight being released was *fear*. While she would eventually experience the usual grief a widow knows, fear never got a grip on her heart again. "I left fear in the hospital that day," she recalled, "and I know it was because I was obedient to praise the Lord and trust Him with my future."

When she went into her husband's hospital room after shedding her fear, one of his former classmates was visiting him. Lena could never have imagined that five years later that man would become her second husband after they met again at a class reunion. In fact, she never expected to marry again; but they have enjoyed seventeen happy years together now.

Can you give God your "what-ifs" of fear and trust Him with them? My list was mighty long at first. At night I lay awake thinking of all the terrible what-ifs that might happen to me now that I was flying solo. It took me a while to deal with those fears, each in turn. Some I had no control over, some I could address directly. Others turned out to be little annoyances, not the big giants I had imagined. What about you?

Scripture

For you did not receive a spirit that makes you a slave again to fear, but you received the Spirit of sonship. And by him we cry, "Abba, Father." The Spirit himself testifies with our spirit that we are God's children. *(Romans 8:15-16 NIV)*

Prayer

Heavenly Father, I choose to cast my fears and anxieties upon You and receive Your comfort and direction. I can think of so many scenarios that start with 'what if?' and my imagination runs away from me. Thank You in advance for delivering me from fretting over things I cannot change. Lord, I want to praise You for rescuing me so many times in the past, and I praise You that even now You are giving me courage to face the future. Amen.

33.

Worry: A Companion to Fear

Fear has a twin called worry. Corrie ten Boom once said, "Worry is a cycle of inefficient thoughts whirling around a center of fear."[8] If I asked when was the last time you worried, you might just say, "Today!"

Jesus' instruction to us is clear: "Therefore I say to you, do not worry about your life . . . Do not worry about tomorrow, for tomorrow will worry about its own things. Sufficient for the day is its own trouble" (Matthew 6: 25, 34).

One commentator writes, "Worry means 'to divide into parts.' The word suggests a distraction, a preoccupation with things causing anxiety, stress, and pressure. Jesus speaks against worry and anxiety because of the watchful care of a heavenly Father who is ever mindful of our daily needs."[9]

Worry comes in all sizes. There are the "biggies," including:

- Money: how will I pay for the extra house repairs?
- Health: who will take care of me as my arthritis gets worse?
- Living choices: if I move across country to be close to my children, will their families even have time for me? Will anyone buy my house, when I don't have the money to fix it up?

I once read an article entitled "Wait to Worry," which included results of a survey of four thousand worriers. Some of the findings amazed me:

- 40 percent of the things people worry about have already happened, so they can do nothing about them.
- Another 30 percent of what they worry about could never happen.
- 22 percent of what they worry about, if it comes, will have so little effect that it isn't worth worrying about.
- By process of elimination, only 8 percent of our worries are "worth the worry."[10]

Have you thought about speaking Scriptures out loud to help faith override worry? The Bible says: "So then faith comes by hearing, and hearing by the word of God" (Romans 10:17). When I hear my own voice reiterating what the Bible says about me as one of God's children, it truly builds my trust. For example, if I am worried about a big decision I have to make today, I might paraphrase Scripture to form a prayer:

> Lord, Your word says that You will accomplish what concerns me—You will fulfill Your purpose for me. I believe it, and I expect Your intervention today in this situation I am facing. Work out all the details. Thank You in advance. I choose to cast my worry on You (see Psalm 138:8).

I also like to post encouraging Scriptures around my house so that throughout the day I can see them, repeat them aloud, and, eventually, memorize them. Maybe you have discovered a special way to get rid of your worry.

Scripture

So shall My word be that goes forth from My mouth; it shall not return to Me void, But it shall accomplish what I please, And it shall prosper in the thing for which I sent it, for you shall go out with joy, and be led out with peace. (Isaiah 55:11-12)

Prayer

Lord, I admit it—I worry too much. I yearn to come to the place of total abandonment where I can be worry-free because I have such complete trust in You. Thank You, heavenly Father, that You know all the things I need. I pray in Jesus' name. Amen.

34.

Overcoming Guilt

Many widows experience some type of guilt, and one author describes three phases they often go through:

> *Phase One*—The widow feels guilty about being alive, or about what she might have done—if not to change the outcome, then at least to have mitigated a detail or event. Given another opportunity, there is always something that could have been done differently and maybe with different results. (As she gets on with her life, she will go through the next phases).
>
> *Phase Two*—She feels ill at ease about spending money, or ignoring what might have been his wishes. In general, managing some kind of transition into widowhood is Phase Two guilt.
>
> *Phase Three*—Guilt occurs when, moving along, finding satisfaction in her ability to cope, and taking some pride in surmounting unfair and uneven odds, the widow takes on a kind of "Look, No Hands" pride that is tinged with uneasiness as well as guilt.[11]

Guilt plagued me for weeks; I felt like I didn't do enough as my husband's caregiver for the long months he was ill. In reality, I was often exhausted and ran short of patience. I felt guilt for not doing things I should have recognized. Where was my discernment? Why didn't I insist the doctors call in more specialists? Why didn't I do this or that?

My feelings were akin to David's when he wrote: "My guilt has overwhelmed me like a burden too heavy to bear" (Psalm 38: 4 NIV).

A friend shared a similar guilt. "My husband would not wear the hearing aids we bought, because he hated them. So I struggled to speak louder, usually getting mad and having a tone of voice that was anything but pleasant. I guess we expect ourselves to be better than we are, setting such high standards and forgetting that we really are human. Now, don't let the devil sabotage you with guilt. And don't be so hard on yourself. You have enough grief as is. You are worn out physically and are emotionally drained. You need much rest and healing. The guilt will eventually leave as you release it to the Lord. You can overcome this. I promise you."

You may be going through a different kind of guilt. Maybe you feel guilty because you don't think you deserve the money left to you. Or your children make you feel guilty on how you spend it. Or you have allowed guilt to overrule your good judgment in decisions you have made.

When guilt tries to rob me of peace, especially when scenes from my husband's last illness taunt me, I stop and have a little talk with the Lord. I ask Him to take my guilty feelings and get rid of them forever.

Scripture

When He [Jesus] had by offering Himself accomplished our cleansing of sins and riddance of guilt, He sat down at the right hand of the divine Majesty on high. (Hebrews 1:3b AMP)

Prayer

Lord Christ, when I felt guilty I am reminded that on the cross You not only paid the price for my sins, but also took my guilt by dying in my place. So now I free myself from guilt. Help me to remember the good things I did to make my husband comfortable. I am grateful, Lord, for what You have done for me. Amen.

35.

Looking Ahead, Setting Goals

As you move forward toward healing and wholeness, ask yourself some questions: "What new goals can I aim for? What do I want to happen? This week? Next month? Next year?"

Several widows made suggestions for setting realistic goals to achieve a healthy balance:

- Take care of yourself.
- Get adequate sleep and exercise.
- Eat healthy food.
- Make regular doctor appointments and keep them.
- Consider joining a support group for widows, preferably through a church.
- Expand your social circles, meeting new people—but be careful about going after a "boyfriend" too soon.
- Create a financial plan that you can live on, and get a professional or trusted friend to help you.
- Be careful about selecting someone who sells financial products and might view vulnerable widows as easy targets.
- Think about writing a legacy letter to your kids with your beliefs, values, and hopes for their generation.

- Consider restarting an old hobby, or starting a new one.
- Take time for yourself to do something fun, maybe taking a trip for a change of scenery, or exploring local places of special interest to you.
- Volunteer.
- Join an intercessory prayer team.

I hope you too will find encouragement in what this teacher wrote:

> My expectations in uncertain times are best described in two words—surprise and creativity. I believe God is going to open new doors of surprise. His strategic positioning will continue, but the way in which He does it will be creative, resulting in smiles and affirmation that He alone is the living God. Divine appointments, open doors, and new ideas will bring about His purposes and plan. Something great is beginning to mount, and there is no summit too high—too impossible—with our God.[12]

What surprises do you suppose the Lord has waiting for you? He says to ask in faith (Mark 11:22-25). Now let's begin to embrace the new season God has for us.

Scripture

Wait for the Lord; be strong and take heart and wait for the Lord.
(Psalm 27:14 NIV)

Prayer

Thank You, Lord, that I can plant hope and expectations into my heart and trust You for the seeds to grow big. You say if I have faith even as a mustard seed, it will grow! So take my tiny faith and do a miracle for me. Favor! Grace! I need a big dose of favor and grace today, Lord. Help me begin to envision my future, to set attainable goals. Amen.

36.

Encouraged by Answered Prayer

Can you remember a prayer God answered for you? Did it happen "suddenly," after you had almost given up waiting? Recalling such incidences bolsters our assurance that He is still in the prayer-answering business. Many widows find that remembering answered prayers helps them push back discouragement when they are most vulnerable. Maggie sent me a poignant reminder of this:

> My husband, Chris, and I used to pray each evening together. This is part of what I miss immensely now that he is gone. He never failed to ask our heavenly Father to draw his brother back to Himself. He realized only God understood what had caused the initial pain, bitterness, and hardness his brother harbored toward the Lord.
>
> But, miracle of miracles, at Chris's memorial service, his brother came back to the Lord! He was a changed man when he left. He told everyone about God, even said to me in the midst of my grieving, "Maggie, you aren't alone. God is with you." A month later, he died unexpectedly. I know my husband's deepest prayer was answered for his brother, and now they are both with

> Jesus. When I get discouraged, I think of all the times God has answered prayer and I know He will answer mine for guidance through my years ahead as a widow.

Maybe it's time for you to go over in your mind significant answers to prayer you have experienced; ones that will be a springboard for encouragement to replace your discouragement!

Scripture

Confess to one another therefore your faults and pray [also] for one another, that you may be healed and restored [to a spiritual tone of mind and heart]. The earnest (heartfelt, continued) prayer of a righteous man makes tremendous power available [dynamic in its working]. (James 5:16 AMP)

Prayer

Father, thank You for reminding me of all the times You heard and answered my prayers in the past. Thank You that I can rely on You for all I need. Put me on the heart of those friends who will stand in the gap for me with effective prayer. Amen.

37.

Full-time Service

An elderly widow named Anna had the privilege of being among the first to proclaim Jesus as the Christ, the Redeemer she had long waited to see. Mary and Joseph brought the baby Jesus to the temple in Jerusalem to present Him to the Lord and for Mary's purification rites, required by Jewish law.

Anna had looked for the Redeemer most of her life, spending upward of sixty years in the temple. She had been married only seven years, and then spent her remaining years fasting, praying, and worshipping God in the temple. In fact, she never left it.

One translation says she talked about the child to all who were waiting expectantly for His birth (see Luke 2:36-38). I have heard her message called one of reconciliation, since Jesus came to reconcile the world to God. It is hard to imagine one such as Anna living a solitary life for so long, but she was privileged to see her prayers answered in the very person of the baby Jesus.

Through the ages, Anna has been an example to many widows who have dedicated their lives to serve the Lord in round-the-clock service, many in lands far from home—some in full-time ministry, others answering God's call in various occupations.

One name stands out to me: Elisabeth Elliot. She and her husband, Jim, lived in Ecuador, where the Elliot's and other missionaries hoped to bring Christ to the Auca Indians by translating the gospel for this violent tribe. In January 1956, when Jim Elliot and four other missionaries attempted to reach some of these Auca Indians, they were murdered.

Can you imagine what emotions Elisabeth could have felt over the injustice of her husband's death? But instead of letting unforgiveness, bitterness, or anger get the best of her, she chose a higher road. Elisabeth continued living in Ecuador, working among the Quichuas Indians. She later lived and worked among the Aucas with Rachel Saint, older sister of Nate Saint, who was also killed alongside Jim.

Elisabeth returned to the States and wrote a heartwarming book about the conversion of this once-savage tribe. Nine years after the men were slain, the Gospel of Mark was published in the Auca language and many of them became Christians. God had used these women, a widow and a sister of the murdered missionaries, to help bring the Aucas reconciliation and salvation through Christ.[13]

Elisabeth has since reached hundreds of thousands of people through her inspirational books and radio lectures. She was widowed once more, and then remarried. Here is something she wrote in *Love Has a Price Tag*:

> The principles of gain through loss, of joy through sorrow, of getting by giving, of fulfillment by laying down, of life out of death is what that Book [the Bible] teaches, and the people who have believed it enough to live it out in simple, humble, day-by-day practice are people who have found the gain, the joy, the getting, the fulfillment, the life. I really do believe that. Lord, help me to live it out.[14]

Scripture

Now all things are of God, who has reconciled us to Himself through Jesus Christ, and has given us the ministry of reconciliation, that is, that God was in Christ reconciling the world to Himself, not imputing their trespasses to them, and has committed to us the word of reconciliation. Now then, we are ambassadors for Christ, as though God were pleading through us: we implore you on Christ's behalf, be reconciled to God. (2 Corinthians 5:18-20)

Prayer

God, begin to show me clearly what Your role is for me in Your Kingdom's work. Even though I may not go into full-time ministry, I can serve as Your hands extended to others in a variety of ways. Show me how. Amen.

Part Four

Embracing a New Season

38.

Accepting the New You

As we shift into this new era of "growing single," as one widow called it, we will discover things we did not know about ourselves. Miriam Neff wrote as she was on her journey:

> As surely as *vulnerable* describes us, so does strength. Look with me at our new boldness, our new freedom and flexibility, and our new ability to comfort others. We are forced to change because the world as we knew it shifted dramatically . . . We have to reach for resources we never knew we had, skills within that have never been needed, and hope within, in order to face each new day. We catch a glimpse of the new person in the mirror and whisper to her, "I didn't know you could."[1]

Becoming a widow means our other half is now gone. You may be a daughter, sister, aunt, sister-in-law, grandmother, friend, but no longer a wife. How sad if you saw yourself only as a wife, as wonderful as that privilege was. The truth is, a lot of us gained status through our husbands. Now we must form an identity all on our own, if we hadn't before. One widow calls this new season a time of discovering our "selfhood."

You might even identify with June. A few weeks after her husband's death, she suddenly realized she had lived in his shadow for so long that her own personality had almost disappeared. He had been the life of the party, always with a witty story to share, while she was the wallflower sitting quietly by. After he was gone, if someone asked her opinion, she didn't know how to respond. But gradually, June is discovering all sorts of things about herself she had kept hidden. And she enjoys speaking up to give her views.

"It's been a surprise, and liberating to discover who I really am," she said. "I have even started visiting those from my church who are homebound since many of them enjoy having someone to talk with."

Is this an identity crisis? Not really, especially when we embrace our identity in Christ Himself. Yes, we are no longer wives—a Mrs. linked to her Mr.—but can we get to the place where we say, "I can't change what happened, but by the grace of God I can come through this crisis a stronger woman because of my dependence on the Lord."

In *Finding Hope Again*, Neil Anderson wrote, "Those who find their identity, security, and sense of worth in the natural order of things will lose it . . . Attachments to this world subtract from our attachment to Christ. On the other hand, nothing can separate us from the love of God, and we will suffer no debilitating loss that we cannot endure if we find our life, identity, acceptance, security, and significance in Christ."[2]

We have the promises of God to tell us who we really are. You might start a list:

- I am a daughter of the King of Kings and Lord of Lords (see I Timothy 6:15)
- I am an overcomer (see John 16:32-33)
- I am a victor, not a victim (see Romans 8:37)
- I can do all things through Christ who strengthens me (Philippians 4:13)
- Add more as you read the Bible yourself.

Scripture

For we are His workmanship, created in Christ Jesus for good works, which God prepared beforehand that we should walk in them. (Ephesians 2:10)

Prayer

Lord, I ask You to restore my authentic self, that self I don't really know. In times when I become vulnerable, I am counting on You to keep me from experiencing low self-esteem. I want to place my identity in You. Help me discover new strengths and give me holy boldness for my new life ahead. Thank You that I am Your workmanship! Amen.

39.

The Choice of Remarriage

Judith gained a new lease on life more quickly than she ever imagined. When her husband of fifty years died, she spent the first year doing what she calls "every active thing I could find." That meant serving in her church, visiting with friends, and taking two trips overseas—all in the first year.

> I guess I was postponing the grief process, but I had grieved so much before my husband died that I just didn't let the tears come right away. By the second year I felt lost, lonely. I was attending a care group in my church and a widower named John soon offered to pick me up for the meetings. Before long, he was driving me to church. Then we were officially dating, going to restaurants and fun places.
>
> Four months later, we married. I am so happy—simply overjoyed. My first husband was retired military, a bookworm who didn't like to go out much. John loves to go places as much as I do. He still works four days a week, but on long weekends we often visit his children or mine (we each have four). I have more freedom than I have ever had. John is so easy to love, and he laughs a lot. We have the same friends through church. He sold his house and

> moved into mine because it is larger. I don't even want to think what my life would be like living in this house alone, now that I have experienced what love is like the second time around. I am glad I made this decision, because I know the Lord guided us both.

Judith is among a smaller percentage of older widows who remarry. Someone said dating among older women is often described as "someone to go out with" rather than "someone to come home to." But of course, each widow must make the choice that best fits her personality and heart's desire.

Lillian married her college sweetheart too soon after her husband's death—at least her adult children thought so. Several still aren't even speaking to her. However, they all knew what an abusive marriage she had endured. She is happily married now and has no regrets, and feels the children will change their minds in time.

Rosie, on the other hand, decided not to marry again after dating a former classmate long-distance for five years. They were reacquainted when she had been a widow for one year, when she returned to her home state to attend her class reunion. He was not as flexible as she wished. She could not see herself moving across country, leaving her children and grandchildren behind. She would have preferred dividing their time between both their homes, say winters in her Florida townhouse and summers at his Wyoming place. But he gave an ultimatum—move to where he lived or else. She chose to stay single, though she was heartbroken over their breakup.

If you believe remarriage is God's best for you, ask Him to direct your steps and bring you across the path of the right man in the right time. Can you be content if He doesn't desire that for you right now?

Scripture

A man's heart plans his way, But the Lord directs his steps.
(Proverbs 16:9)

Prayer

Father, I am lonesome. You know how to best fill that void. Please bring the people of Your choosing into my life. Keep me from being deceived. I want only Your plan for me. Amen.

40.

Happily ever after! That's how the fairy tales end. But is that reality?

At our wedding, most of us took vows to be true "until death do us part," but our star-studded eyes never envisioned the day when our prince would not be by our side. Suddenly we are alone, and widowed. Can we love again? Here's the story of one who did:

> I had reached a stage of contentment—finally. I was actually relived that my craziness was gone. I felt normal again, sort of. I could read a book again with focus. I was now resigned to be by myself rather than dating, after a disappointing experience. I had fallen for a guy who was attractive, a perfect gentleman with a sharp mind, but a double-minded one. I later learned he was dating me to make his real girlfriend jealous. The disaster lasted four months and I finally broke it off after my daughters confronted me and showed me what a manipulator he was. When I did fall in love again, if I ever did, I wanted to be one with my husband. In the meantime, I'd be content.

Two years after my husband of twenty-five years had died, I met William. It was such a spiritual experience, I can hardly describe it. We had both lost spouses and were comforted by each other's physical presence. We had a passionate honeymoon. Today, it is so good to have someone in the house to talk with, watch a movie with, and go to dinner with. He knew my mom for six years before she died. Four grandchildren have been born since we married, so he is their grandpa. We both knew all the same church folks, even some old school friends. We've been through at least twenty deaths of family and friends, and some serious illnesses with my children.

Life would have been a lot harder bearing all that alone. I am grateful to God for our blended family. It is like William was always there. I guess my needs finally overruled my fears about remarriage. But I think I had to get to the place of contentment first.

My neighbor who remarried told me the second time around is like having a second child. You don't love the first one any less; you have plenty of love for another baby. You just enjoy and love them differently. So it is with your new husband. I found it to be so.

Yes, some widows truly find love the second time around. Three of my close friends have, and I rejoice at their newfound happiness. I enjoy being around them because they are so "giddy in love." But the truth is that some widows do not find it, and others don't even want it. For those who do, we are glad for them.

Scripture

Who can find a virtuous wife? For her worth is far above rubies. The heart of her husband safely trusts her; so he will have no lack of gain. She does him good and not evil all the days of her life.
(Proverbs 31:10-12)

Prayer

Thank You, Lord, for my second chance at love. I never knew it was possible, but You saw my need and helped him find me. What an awesome Father You are. Help me to always be a good wife to him. Thank You for the fun times we enjoy together, and for blending our two families. Amen.

41.

Learning Contentment

Is *contentment* an elusive dream you think you will never know? If so, you have joined the ranks of other discontented or lonely widows who have also wondered. Most of us have been at that place, if we are honest. Please don't throw in the towel just yet. Are you at least willing to allow God to deal with your discontentment? Jessie did.

Jessie was widowed at the age of twenty-three when her pastor-husband was killed in a car crash. With two young daughters to raise, she decided to move back to her childhood home where she had parents and grandparents to help her. She got a job, established a routine, but still Jessie was lonely.

One night, when she told God how unhappy she was, she heard Him reply, "You don't have to be happy, but you can be content."

"That did it!" she says. "From that day, I asked the Lord to work contentment in me. And through the years when things would upset me, God gave me the contentment I needed to get through whatever situation I was in."

Jessie, who had often prayed for another husband, changed her prayer: "God, I am content. If it is your plan for me to marry, you can bring a man into my life; if not, I won't ask again." And she didn't. After seventeen years of widowhood, God sent Addison as a gift to her—as her husband. Ironically, she met him when she took her eldest off to college. They enjoyed a blessed marriage that lasted for forty-five years.[3]

Today, Jessie is a recent widow again. But the lessons she learned long ago about contentment still hold true in her mind-set. She finds joy in living with her daughter's family, and playing with her great-grandchildren when they visit often.

Sometimes God leads us into a decision where we experience fulfillment and joy as a result of our obedience. Other times we may have to make decisions that might cause us to give up some things for a greater good. Or He may even ask us to make a decision without resolving all the problems we face.

So we move ahead believing He is leading us. Yes, we widows will undoubtedly face trying times, requiring us to listen to and trust God to help us through them. And in the middle of it all, we might really discover that seemingly elusive contentment can be ours.

Think about a time when you knew complete contentment. Maybe right now you need a big dose of it. Why not stop and ask God to help you come to that place? It may not be an overnight miracle, but it can come. Perhaps even in a completely unexpected and surprising manner.

Scripture

[Growing in grace] they shall still bring forth fruit in old age; they shall be full of sap [of spiritual vitality] and [rich in the] verdure [of trust, love, and contentment]. (Psalm 92:14 AMP)

Prayer

I want to learn to be content. But I look around me at others and when I get my eyes off You, I get jealous or fall into self-pity. Help me release my own desires and expectations to You. I declare Your lordship over my life. I choose to believe that You will work all my circumstances out to Your best plan. I believe You are working in people and events in a way that ultimately will bring You glory, and work to my good. Amen.

42.

When Children Cause Heartache

Heartache can ensue when adult children do not agree with Dad's wishes being carried out, whether it was in his will or a letter to you, his wife.

Doris' stepchildren resented her even after she had been married to their father for twenty-two years. When her husband knew he was dying, he told Doris, "You will be well taken care of. Don't worry; I have made sure of that. I have left it all to you." Soon those words would haunt her.

A son who received nothing from his dad sued her because he wanted the house where he grew up. Obviously, his daddy knew his son did not know how to manage money, let alone the family home. After months of negotiations between lawyers, Doris settled with her stepson out of court.

As soon as she became a widow, Doris faced another giant hurdle simply because her husband had not shared business procedures with her. In fact, she didn't even know where the paperwork was kept. Step by step, she taught herself. She did well, though it took a while.

After Doris got her business affairs in order, she finally decided she was ready to relocate. She bought a townhouse in another state to be close to her own son's family. Barely settled, she joined an online dating service. Then a surprise—she met a new love. The courtship led to marriage and a move to the town where he lived.

Her journey is an example of a two-fold dilemma many other widows share. If a husband fails to explain the family's financial workings, the survivor must learn those ropes later on her own. Then there is the mistreatment she sometimes suffers when children object to their dad's will. Widows sometimes endure an onslaught from children—bitterness, jealousy, anger, exchange of harsh words, and even lawsuits. All of this adds further to the widow's emotional roller-coaster ride. While Doris's story has a happier ending than some, her early widowhood journey illustrates how desperately we need the Lord as our defender and shield.

Scripture

O Sovereign Lord, my strong deliverer, who shields my head in the day of battle—do not grant the wicked their desires, O Lord, do not let their plans succeed. (Psalm 140:7-8 NIV)

Prayer

Lord, I am glad You are my Defender. You will come to my aid. When I have to wade through a sea of undeserved accusations, You help me. No, I do not deserve this unjust and downright mean treatment. Help me not to cave in if I tend to feel guilty, or give in to threats from those who are after the assets my husband intended for me to have. How I need wisdom and discernment that only You can give me. Thank You, Father, for watching over my financial affairs as well as my physical and emotional well-being. Amen.

43.

The Lord, My Husband

Have you ever had a comforting dream about your deceased spouse? Many widows do. While I never have, I did have a significant dream that impacted me greatly.

In my dream, I climbed some winding stairs to reach the tower in a white ancient looking fortress. Jesus Himself was there waiting, dressed in white and wearing a big grin. He hugged me, took my left hand, and placed a diamond ring on my "marriage" finger. When I got out of bed, I pondered the dream for a while. I knew there was a passage in Isaiah about the Lord being my husband, so I looked it up.

> "Do not fear, for you will not be ashamed; neither be disgraced, for you will not be put to shame; for you will forget the shame of your youth, and will not remember the reproach of your widowhood anymore. For your Maker is your husband, the Lord of hosts is His name; and your Redeemer is the Holy One of Israel. He is called the God of the whole earth. For the Lord has called you like a woman forsaken and grieved in spirit . . . But with everlasting kindness I will have mercy on you," says the Lord, your Redeemer. (Isaiah 54:4-6, 8)

In my Bible, the study notes indicate that God is talking about His relationship with His Israelite people, referring both to their bondage in Egypt and their Babylonian captivity.[4]

But I took this Scripture personally, believing that He was taking away my feelings of reproach as a widow and that He, my Maker, was indeed my Husband.

Also, the fortress where He met me in my dream spoke volumes to me. Many Old Testament scriptures talk about God being our fortress or refuge. One of them is found in Proverbs 14:26: "And His children will have a place of refuge." Refuge here means fortress!

Other places where this Hebrew word *machseh* is used, it means trust—trust in the Lord. He will shelter you from storms, provide a shade in the heat.[5]

Have you seen Him this way in your life yet? As Husband? Provider? Protector? Redeemer? Have you come to a place of such total trust that you will turn to Him to shelter you from the storms that ensue during your widowhood adjustments? If not, you might want to stop right now and talk to Him about it.

Scripture

Because you have made the Lord, who is my refuge, even the Most High, your dwelling place, no evil shall befall you, nor shall any plague come near your dwelling. (Psalm 91:9)

Prayer

Father, when things around me seem to be coming apart, help me take my refuge in You. You are my fortress, shelter, protector. Thank You, my Maker, for being my Husband and helping me get through the myriad of matters facing me. I love You, Lord. Amen.

44.

My new friend Kattie shared with me how she and her high school sweetheart married right after graduation. Soon they had three children and she was a happy homemaker, though she longed to go to college like her husband.

One day, he encouraged her to go to university and get her degree. "You might need to teach someday," he said many times. So she balanced home life with college life and graduated with qualifications to teach English, Latin, and Spanish. Then her husband, a heavy smoker, died at age thirty-eight. But by the time she was widowed, she was a full-time teacher.

After being a widow sixteen years, she married a fellow teacher, a retired military officer. He had been a widower only two years when they married, and his two children just could not accept her, especially after she moved into his home.

Then Hurricane Ivan swept through Florida with great fury, completely destroying their Gulf-front home. Most all the house's contents were washed away, including her expensive collection of books. For the next two years, Kattie and her husband lived in a rented apartment, waiting for the insurance settlement, and the eventual rebuilding of their house. In the meantime, she continued teaching. Finally, they were able to rebuild a dream house on the same Gulf site—a structure capable of withstanding winds up to 145 miles per hour, built on stilts with an elevator to the living area.

Suddenly, after fifteen years of marriage, Kattie could experience a "start-over." This house would reflect more of her personality and not be the same home her husband's children considered theirs. She had a great time furnishing it from garage sales and auctions, expressing her tastes, styles, and colors.

"I sometimes wonder if I made the right decision to marry again, because his children have never accepted me, and that proved a barrier in my marriage," Kattie admitted. "But I have had some happy times. When we walk the beach together in the evening, or watch the sunrise over the Gulf of Mexico in the morning, I realize what I would have missed if I had just lived alone among my books."

While none of our experiences are alike, all of us have an opportunity to start over in some area of our lives: redecorating one room or a whole house; deciding to start a new career or more training; taking a trip; or beginning a new hobby.

Begin to think of ways you want to change something in your life. What have you stored in the back of your mind for a while? Why not decide to try just one creative thing?

Scripture

Because of the Lord's great love we are not consumed, for his compassions never fail. They are new every morning; great is your faithfulness. I say to myself, "The Lord is my portion; therefore I will wait for him." The Lord is good to those whose hope is in him, to the one who seeks him. (Lamentations 3:22-25 NIV*)*

Prayer

Lord, show me what I can change that will bring me enjoyment and some fulfillment. Then help me achieve it. Thank You in advance for doing this. Amen.

45.

Widow's Offering

Giving can be an act of worship. It blesses God. It blesses others. It blesses the giver. While embracing our new "me," we may have a tendency to forget that our God is pleased when we show Him our love and devotion. One way is to give offerings to Him.

On my bedside table, I keep a small metal coin, supposedly a likeness of the coin called a mite in New Testament times. It reminds me that even when my finances shrink, I am still to give to God's kingdom.

One of the stories in the Bible depicts a poor widow whom Jesus commends for her giving. Jesus is teaching in the temple courts, warning against those who seek places of honor at feasts, but devour widows' houses and make long prayers to impress. As people come forward to give their offerings, Jesus observes, and the Scripture records:

> Jesus sat down opposite the place where the offerings were put and watched the crowd putting their money into the temple treasury. Many rich people threw in large amounts. But a poor widow came and put in two very small copper coins [mites], worth only a fraction of a penny. Calling his disciples to him,

> Jesus said, "I tell you the truth, this poor widow has put more into the treasury than all the others. They all gave out of their wealth; but she, out of her poverty, put in everything—all she had to live on" (Mark 12:41-44 NIV).

We know little about this widow except her poverty and her great faith. As my friend Ann Spangler points out:

> But there is yet another more subtle aspect to her story. How easy it would have been for her to conclude that her gift was simply too meager to offer. What need had God for two copper coins anyway? Somehow she must have had the grace to believe in the value of her small offering . . . Her story reminds us that God's kingdom works on entirely different principles than the kingdom of this world. In the divine economy, the size of the gift is of no consequence; what matters is the size of the giver's heart.[6]

Maybe you have experienced times when you thought you just did not have enough money to tithe or to give offerings. God says when we tithe—give a tenth of our income—He opens the windows of heaven and pours out overflowing blessings.

One fall, our pastor asked church members to seek God's will regarding how much each of us should give for an upcoming Christmas offering in support of an orphanage. A widow named Helen lived on a meager pension with no extras to give. But she wrote down $200 on a piece of paper and every day waved it toward heaven, thanking God that by Christmas she would have that amount to give.

While rummaging around in her attic one day, she found a small round box labeled "electrical tape." So she brought it down, thinking she might have use for it. When she opened the box, she was in for a big surprise. There was $200 tucked inside. Her husband had been dead some five years, but she guessed that he had stashed it there for a rainy day.

In church that Christmas Sunday, she held up the little box with the $200 and told her story to our congregation. I don't know who was more excited, the poor widow dropping her offering in the basket, or those of us in the audience clapping for such wonderful provision.

We can ask God what and how to give in our current circumstances. He will guide us. And He may just provide for us in a surprising way.

Scripture

"Bring the whole tithe into the storehouse, so that there may be food in My house, and test Me now in this," says the Lord of hosts, "if I will not open for you the windows of heaven, and pour out for you a blessing until it overflows. Then I will rebuke the devourer for you."
(Malachi 3:10-11 NASB)

Prayer

Lord, though my giving seems so small, much like the widow's mite, take and multiply it to Your service. You know my heart is to give. I know You are the One who enables me to get money, and it really belongs to You anyway—so I am just giving back a portion to You. Amen.

46.

Focus On Helping Others

Are you at a stage where you are now ready to think about helping others, shifting your focus for a while to someone else? If not, it's okay! Don't let guilt rush your healing. But if you are ready to begin moving outward again, consider this . . .

Step into the pages of the New Testament and take a look at Eunice and Lois, a mother and grandmother who brought up young Timothy in the Christian faith.

The apostle Paul referred to him as "my dearly beloved son," and Timothy was associated with Paul in his ministry more than any other companion. Paul addresses two of his letters to Timothy and makes mention of him in other New Testament letters.

Think about it. Timothy's Christian training and influence came from two women, one or maybe both of whom were widows. Perhaps his mother worked and his grandmother cared for him in her absence. We don't know. We are told his father was Greek, so there is conjecture that he was either a non-believer, or died early in Timothy's life. While we have no details about his biological father, Paul considered Timothy his own spiritual son.

As a widow in the 21st century, how can the story of Lois and Eunice apply to you? You may be at a point in your healing where you are ready to reach out and impart your knowledge or experience to your own grandchildren, or some other young person. Maybe you have a talent you can share—in art, music, or writing. Maybe you can tutor schoolchildren; or offer hospitality to some neighborhood kids, college students, or young moms. The possibilities are unlimited. Just think about your own talents and how you can impart them.

Many grandmothers have left their own comfortable homes to move across country to be closer to their children and grandchildren. Yes, some widows relocate so their families can provide care for them during their latter years. Yet, as widows, many use their move as an opportunity to influence a younger generation.

Recently, I talked to a widow of three years who is selling her home and relocating near her daughter in another state. She has three immediate goals in mind. First, she is excited because she will be able to attend her two grandsons' sporting and musical events, and to cheer them on. Second, she wants to share her Christian faith with them, primarily through her life example, by spending quality time with them. Third, she wants to use her interior-design talents to help younger women redecorate their homes, without charge to them. It's what she enjoys.

Helping others, whether they are our grandchildren or others, causes us to take our minds off ourselves. It's awesome to realize that our influence can have eternal value to the people in whom we invest time.

As Eunice and Lois imparted their Christian faith to their young charge, we too can invest in someone else's future. Maybe you want to stop now and ask God to show you what you can contribute, and how you can do it.

Scripture

I thank God, whom I serve with a pure conscience, as my forefathers did, as without ceasing I remember you in my prayers night and day, greatly desiring to see you, being mindful of your tears, that I may be filled with joy, when I call to remembrance the genuine faith that is in you, which dwelt first in your grandmother Lois and your mother Eunice, and I am persuaded is in you also. Therefore I remind you to stir up the gift of God which is in you through the laying on of my hands. For God has not given us a spirit of fear, but of power and of love and of a sound mind. (2 Timothy 1:3-7)

Prayer

Father, God, please stir up the gift that is in me and help me know exactly what it is that You want me to share with someone. Give me the courage to do it. Help me to do it without fear, and out of love. Don't let me be bashful about sharing my faith when the opportunity arises. I thank You in advance for helping me to embrace this new phase of my life. Amen.

Part Five

Renewing Hope in My Heart

47.

Expectations for More Than Enough

Hope deferred does make the heart grow sick. When you reach this stage in your widowhood, it may help to concentrate on some declarations you know are God-ordered.

In his book *Tell Your Heart to Beat Again*, my former pastor Dutch Sheets talks about expectations you can anticipate when you need renewed hope. I excerpted some declarations to repeat aloud—to plant hope in my heart. I hope they encourage you too.

Declaration of Expectations

My *expectation* is to have more than enough:

I expect poverty to break off me. I expect God's provisions and resources to be released to me in great measure.

I expect and anticipate the arrival of abundance.

I expect the favor of the Lord to come upon me.

I expect God's favor in every aspect of my life (family, health, business endeavors, relationships). Lord, open doors, bring contacts that I need and prepare the way before me.

I expect angelic protection!

I expect angels to invade my prison of hope-deferred bondage and release me (Acts 12:7).

I expect my night to give way to light.

I expect the light of hope to break forth as the dawn. I will not be held captive by oppression, discouragement, and depression. This is my point of release.

I expect my chains to fall off (Acts 12:7).

I expect the authority of the Lord to be released in my life. The gates of hell will no longer prevail against me (Matt 16:18). The King of Glory is opening the gate of hope to me. He is coming into my home, family, and life.

I expect the Word of the Lord to prosper in me.

I expect the Word of the Lord over my city and nation to increase.

I expect promises from Scripture to come to pass in my life.

I expect the God of hope to fill me with joy and peace and I will abound in hope (Rom.15:13).

I expect my heart to get well.

I expect the clouds of doubt to yield to the dawn of hope.

I expect a new beginning in my life.

I expect to enjoy life again. I expect to win.

I expect![1]

Consider what He thinks about you. The psalmist encouraged us to "Wait and hope for and expect the Lord" (27:14 AMP). Let's trust Him with our present and our future. And not only do we plant hopes, but we expect them to bear fruit.

Scripture

Many, O Lord my God, are the wonders you have done. The things you planned for us no one can recount to you; were I to speak and tell of them, they would be too many to declare. (Psalm 40:5 NIV*)*

Prayer

Lord, thank You for building hope in my heart. I want to anticipate and expect marvelous things from Your loving hand. Help me not to get impatient but to wait for Your perfect timing. I ask in Jesus' name. Amen.

48.

When You've Lost Hope

Take a look into a window of my soul when one morning I was most discouraged, recovering from a long bout of pneumonia, and crying over mounting bills. I imagine you have experienced similar despair at least one time—perhaps many times. In my journal, I wrote:

> I have lost my hope! I cannot find it in the Bible today. Or in a friend's letter. Or in my own remembrances. It is lost. I don't even want to pursue it. My mountains look so impossible. My health challenges so great. God, help!

I called a prayer partner in another state who is recovering from cancer. After she prayed for me, I felt better. The next morning during my quiet time, I found my answer to recovering hope. In Hosea 2:15, it says, in essence, that God will transform the Valley of Achor into the door of hope. Achor means trouble. Then this explanation struck me: This Hebrew word for hope here also means "expectation, something for which one waits," and "to look hopefully in a particular direction." Its original meaning was "to stretch like a rope." It occurs thirty-three times in Scripture. Yahweh Himself is the hope of the godly. Hope: to stretch like a rope![2]

Seemingly, this passage had nothing to do with my situation or my need for divine intervention—yet it spoke volumes to me. My reason for regaining hope is based upon who God Almighty is and what He has promised in His Word to do: Reverse my trouble!

Then the next passage said, "In that day," declares the Lord, "you will call me 'my husband' . . . " (Hosea 2:16 NIV).

Are you ready for hope to lasso in your discouragement? Are you ready to trust Him completely? It is not always easy, of course. But are you willing to start? I hope so.

Scripture

For You are my hope, O LORD GOD; You are my trust from my youth. By You I have been upheld from birth; You are He who took me out of my mother's womb. My praise shall be continually of You. I have become as a wonder to many, but You are my strong refuge. Let my mouth be filled with Your praise and with Your glory all the day. Do not cast me off in the time of old age; do not forsake me when my strength fails . . . But I will hope continually, and will praise You yet more and more." (Psalm 71:5-9, 14)

Prayer

Lord, I choose to let You extend that rope of hope to me. Help me to trust You to reverse my trouble. I am blessed to be able to call You my husband and trust You that You have a solution to my various issues. In fact, You can handle all things that concern me. Thank You, Lord. Amen.

49. Congratulate Yourself

Every now and then, you've got to pat yourself on the back and give yourself a round of applause. Some widows told me they felt congratulations were in order when:

- "I dined alone at our favorite restaurant and didn't cry when the waitress asked where my husband was."
- "I waded through thirteen boxes of his receipts and paperwork, some ten years' worth."
- "I wrote my first check on my own—for electricity."
- "I made my first big solo decision—to pay off the car loan and save $500 by doing it early."
- "I negotiated prices for others to do necessary house improvements (painting the house, mowing the grass, repairing tile, installing a security system, and replacing large kitchen appliances) all within a few weeks of becoming a widow. I also negotiated for new house insurance when mine was canceled."
- "I canceled all the junk mail sent to my husband."
- "I donated to charity his clothes and personal items that the children didn't want."

- "I started sticking to a budget to lessen my stress."
- "I switched all bills and accounts to my name."
- "I applied for my own credit card with my own credit rating."
- "I marked the first anniversary of my husband's passing by planting a tree in our yard with a memorial ceremony, as two young grandchildren told stories about their 'Poppy'."

After we have celebrated, more realization sets in as we discover abilities and skills we didn't know existed. One widow admitted, "I gained an appreciation of my own ability to solve issues."

More questions you may ask yourself: What do I want to do with the rest of my life? Should I get a job? Volunteer? Take up a hobby? Go back to school? Enroll in a gym? Take that long dreamed-of trip? Do I move?

Add your own questions, then schedule some "thinking time" and write down your hopes, dreams, and ideas. Researchers believe when we express concerns on paper, it helps free the brain to concentrate on solutions. Writing in a journal has helped me think more clearly as I weigh the pros and cons of various choices. And of course, it is always good to invite God to help you with these decisions.

Remember: with each decision made, and with each step forward taken, celebrate and congratulate yourself.

Scripture

My soul, wait only upon God and silently submit to Him; for my hope and expectation are from Him. (Psalm 62:5 AMP)

Prayer

Lord, I could not have reached this stage without Your prompting and help. Thank You that the Holy Spirit is my Comforter, Teacher, Enabler, and that He will keep helping me to adjust to my new role. Amen.

50.

Help, God! I'm Human

Do you sometimes think you are temporarily insane? One widow, whose fifty-six-year-old husband died sitting next to her on the couch, wrote me recently:

> When you lose your husband as unexpectedly as I did, you are temporarily insane. You really are—not even able to make any wise choices. A part of your brain dies with your husband—at least for a while.
>
> I attended Grief Share for about a year. Being with other folks with similar losses really helped me put pieces of the puzzle together, as I began to recognize what I was experiencing is normal.
>
> I found out I was not alone, and that God wasn't picking on me. I used to sit in church and feel angry and jealous. I'd think, *"The woman over there still has her husband, who is a jerk, while my godly man is gone. What kind of sadist arranged that?"*
>
> I was really ticked off at God for a while. One night in bed, I was wailing away, asking God why He didn't just take me, too. The phone rang at that moment. It was my husband's brother, Dick. He calmed me down, and talked me through

the feelings of abandonment. This happened several times, his calling just in the nick of time, literally.

Dick was single at the time, teaching in Europe, and he had some free time to take me under his wing. He flew home for the funeral, and was very attentive to me. Something happened that I learned is normal, but nevertheless confusing to a new widow. You can have a transference of affection toward someone who is there for you, very innocently, especially if the death of the spouse is sudden. There is a vacuum that pulls in someone who steps into it. In my case, it was Dick. A long brotherly hug was all it took.

There was a side of my brain that said, "This is crazy." The other side said, "This is comforting." I was in a bubble for about a year with that struggle. I visited Europe to tour with him where he taught. I laughed, cried, and forgot for an hour at a time that I was a widow. The trip was delightfully distracting. I wondered if maybe one day, Dick and I could be a couple. I wouldn't even have to change my name. But he was fifteen years younger. I knew I would not want to someday be eighty, and him just sixty-five.

I started going to a counselor, who helped to sort out my feelings. Eventually I had to work out an escape route. I never really knew if Dick's feelings for me were mutual, but I think they were. We had so much fun together, talking for hours. By the time I made a break from him, I was much more ready to face life alone without my crutch.

But I now tell women to beware of the wolves who prey on attractive wealthy widows. Although Dick's intentions were always honorable, I came to see how vulnerable and easily swayed widows can be. Because my husband had left me well provided for, I could have been taken advantage of by someone.

A few years later, this widow did remarry, but not to her brother- in-law. Her second marriage has been a happy, compatible one. Yet her story has a lesson for us: We must guard against our vulnerability to fall for any man who pays attention to us. We need to ask God for discernment; ask Him if this is a God-sent friend . . . or someone interested in a lustful relationship . . . or someone out for financial gain . . . or a man truly interested in you for the right reasons. Listen for God's warning or an "all-clear" sign to proceed with the friendship.

Scripture

Or do you not know that your body is the temple of the Holy Spirit who is in you, whom you have from God, and you are not your own? For you were bought at a price; therefore glorify God in your body and in your spirit, which are God's. (1 Corinthians 6:19-20)

Prayer

Lord, help me keep a pure heart (and body) in any new relationship I form now. I want to be pleasing to You. Help me remember that my body is the temple of the Holy Spirit, always to be used for Your glory and honor. Amen.

51.

Flee Sexual Fantasies

Women can easily become ensnared in sexual fantasies and be vulnerable to affairs—whether they choose to hang out in ungodly places, or watch X-rated movies or television shows, or use cyberspace to connect to social networks. They can even get a fixation on a man at church—or at the gym or any number of places. Too bad we don't have traffic lights in our life: a flashing yellow that says "Caution," and a red one that clearly indicates, "Stop!" But wait! We do have a built-in warning system—and His name is the Holy Spirit.

More than one widow admitted to me that she had a "knowing-in-her-knower" that she should stop seeing a certain friend, but she had a hard time making a final breakaway.

A young widow told me, "I was very vulnerable to any man's touch, including the fellow who washed my hair before he cut it, and the chiropractor who adjusted my back. They awoke yearnings in me to be held again—to be safe, and to have someone take care of me. I was like a satellite flying erratically out of orbit. Yet I was a Christian and knew sex outside marriage was unacceptable to God."

Christian teacher Judy Reamer talks about mental adultery, which can be a problem for singles as well as for married women. She writes:

> Whether your source of sexual temptation is an old boyfriend, a man on the job, or only someone you have had a dream about, the solution is still the same . . . Improper sexual behavior always starts first in the mind . . . Therefore, while this solution may sound simplistic, it is still the best answer: Stop the thoughts! Nip them in the bud . . . Do not let your imagination run away from you. Choose not to review last night's passionate dream. Occupy your mind with organizing your day. Read the Bible, listen to a program on a Christian radio station, or dig out a new recipe for supper. Before long, the sexual thoughts will dissipate. Remember my little motto: "Affairs start in the head before they get to the bed."[3]

What a truth! You may need to stop right now and pray: "Lord, help me bring my thought life under control. Help me nip those ungodly thoughts in the bud."

Please, dear one, do not allow yourself to believe that an Internet liaison is harmless. Satan can use this deception to destroy your relationship with God. You probably know someone who left his or her family for a stranger she met over the Internet, with disastrous results. Yes, you can possibly meet a Christian mate on the right dating service. I know some single gals and guys who did, and have great marriages. But beware: The highway of life is riddled with disappointment due to wrong choices. Ask God to guide you.

Mary was just forty-seven, the mother of three grown children, when her husband died of cancer. For the next two years, she sat in her "prayer chair" getting to know God better by devouring the Bible. What was His desire for her? She prayed: *"Lord, I have natural human emotions, so I am asking you to put a hedge of protection around my heart. Guard me. I want only Your plan for my life whether I remarry or not."*

Now some twenty-seven years later she has been to nearly forty different nations teaching and praying over those lands. She never did remarry, but has felt fulfilled doing what she calls "His kingdom's work."

Many widows have found that maintaining a vital relationship with Christ fully meets their emotional and spiritual needs. May you discover some truths for yourself as to what God's plan for your future is to include. The precaution bears repeating: don't run ahead of Him. Wait for His peace and direction.

Scripture

Finally, brethren, whatever things are true, whatever things are noble, whatever things are just, whatever things are pure, whatever things are lovely, whatever things are of good report, if there is any virtue and if there is anything praiseworthy—meditate on these things.
(Philippians 4:8)

Prayer

Lord, help me deal the right way with lustful thoughts, runaway fantasies, and sexual dreams. I ask for You to help me to bring these under control, to wipe them away. Please give me the courage to say no when they invade my thought life and tempt me to sin against You and my body, which is the temple of the Holy Spirit. Thank You. Amen.

52.

Undecided About the Future

Patricia had been married for several decades. A year after her husband's death, friends introduced her to a gentleman at a dinner party. Soon he was taking her to eat, and driving her to church. Now they see each other much more frequently.

"Are you considering marriage?"

"Yes," she said, "But after seven years of having him as my boyfriend, I am still undecided."

"Why?"

"Two reasons really. I took care of my sick husband so long I just don't want to have another man to nurse through an illness. Also, I don't want another man to boss me around and not accept me as a woman with a mind of my own who can make decisions. I have enjoyed my independence for these past eight years, though there are times I have been extremely lonely."

Whether there is a new man in your life, or one you have been dating for a while, you too may be undecided or confused about where the relationship should go. Ask the Lord to give you some answers. Ask a trusted friend to listen as you bounce off the "positive" and "negative" issues or concerns you have. Ask God to give you wisdom!

Scripture

But the wisdom that is from above is first pure, then peaceable, gentle, willing to yield, full of mercy and good fruits, without partiality and without hypocrisy. (James 3:17)

Prayer

Lord, there is a special man in my life right now. I need Your help to keep our relationship what You want it to be—no more and no less. I don't know whether what I feel for him is real love or just infatuation springing out of my deep longing for a significant somebody in my life. I am not sure what his intentions are toward me. Lord, keep me from reading into his actions a deeper interest than he really feels. Don't let me miss Your best. Father, I don't want to pursue a relationship that doesn't have Your blessing. Protect my heart, and reveal Your will to me. I ask in Jesus' name. Amen.[4]

53.

Dealing with Loneliness

Of course you have to fight off loneliness now that you are a widow. Loneliness can lead women into relationships that are not healthy; or into depression, as well as any number of poor decisions or wrong behaviors.

Anne, who lost her husband ten years ago wrote, "The agony of aloneness was so wrenching to me at first, the crying so wearying, that I was desperate to move beyond it. I told the Lord, 'Please move me through this as fast as I can possibly stand it.' The pain has lessened. Someone told me, *'You get through it, not over it.'* I think that's true."

But she did make a bad choice early in her widowhood. "One day I remembered a huge mistake or sin I made after I became a widow. Although I had asked for forgiveness, I needed someone to say 'God understands and is embracing you again.' Finally the Lord provided a retreat speaker at my church who listened and pronounced me forgiven. But now I realize that remembering it is a good deterrent to acting like that again. Pain is a good teacher. God is compassionate. Satan is merciless, even to a widow."

Sandy told me she liked her own company so much, she did not experience loneliness after Earl died. We laughed about it at the time, but I never forgot her admonition to like yourself and to try to enjoy your alone time. I hoped someday I'd reach that goal.

Aunt Betty used to talk to the Lord out loud after Uncle Daniel died. One day I heard her asking where to get knitting yarns to make afghans for the unwed mothers' home. I asked if she was talking to me. "Oh, no, I am asking Jesus where I will find the best prices, and if I get quiet He will bring to my mind the name of the right store," she answered. I walked away to let her hear.

When loneliness pangs hit me now, I pick up the phone to talk to a friend or sit at my computer and send some email messages. One of my daily goals is to try to think of one person I can bless. It might be as simple as writing a thank-you letter to let someone know how she or he has impacted my life. I especially enjoy writing older women who have mentored me, pastors who have pastored me, and teachers who have taught me. Then there are the friends I can't forget who have walked through valleys with me. They deserve a note of appreciation now and then.

Of course, the best way to combat loneliness is to curl up with a Bible and read God's love letters to you. Some widows recommend reading from a translation you perhaps might not have read before, such as *The Message*, which is written in everyday English. Of course, this paraphrase is not the route to take when you want to study the Bible.

Then ask the Lord to be there with you.

Scripture

A man [or woman] who has friends must himself [herself] be friendly, but there is a friend who sticks closer than a brother. (Proverbs 18:24)

Prayer

Lord, You know how lonesome I get some days. I need companionship and friendship. I want friends who like being with me just because I'm me. Keep me from being deceived by new acquaintances who may come into my life. Lord, fill the lonely place in my heart. Amen.

54.

Remembering Happy Times

Robbie had been married for ten years, was a stay-at-home mom to three young children, and lived in Europe with her husband, a serviceman in the Air Force. She had come back to the States to help settle things after her father-in-law's death since her husband had to return to duty.

One spring morning a team from the Air Force knocked on her door with the devastating news that her husband was among those killed in a military plane crash. Rescuers were hindered in getting to the site due to bad weather and mountainous terrain, so it was almost a month before his body was returned for burial. Thankfully, she was staying in the same town where her parents lived, so she received their emotional support.

"As an adult, I knew death is part of life, but your children don't know that," Robbie said. "I think the hardest part was dealing with their grief. No one will ever take their dad's place. Knowing that my husband had a personal relationship with the Lord eased my grieving, and I have tried to let my children know the importance of that too."

For Robbie, filling her mind with joyful recollections has helped to work through the grief. "My husband hated for people to be sad," she said. "When I feel sad because he is not here, I think of our good times. I have found that if you let the Lord work through your grief, He can bring you into joy. What you dwell on certainly determines how you feel. I like to be with people who can remind me of happy times, happy thoughts."

It has been seven years since her husband's death. Robbie returned to the work force a year after becoming a widow. Because she lives in a predominately military town, she is also a volunteer on the Air Force base to help other families who are experiencing the grief of losing a loved one. Her sixteen-year-old daughter also helps youngsters who lose a parent. Whenever she can, Robbie tells her children funny things their dad used to say. She wants them to catch his sense of humor too.

After talking to her, I started a list of comical things my children's dad did or said that I can share with them. Maybe you will want to do that also.

Scripture

He will yet fill your mouth with laughter, and your lips with shouts of joy. (Job 8:21 NIV)

Prayer

Lord, thank You that when we are sad, we can recall happy times and know that You will restore our joy! Thank You for the fun times we enjoyed as a family and for the wonderful memories—some of which cause us to laugh hilariously. Amen.

55.

Laughter Restores Joy

Laughter is said to be the best medicine. It is believed to increase job performance, can connect people emotionally, and improves the flow of oxygen to the heart and brain. Laughter can also be a key to unlock our grief, especially if we can learn not to take ourselves too seriously.

Barbara Johnson, the late author and humorist, helped many people on their journey through grief by getting them to laugh. Though well acquainted with grief herself, Barbara was one of the most joyful people I have ever met. In spite of the calamities in her life, she learned to laugh. She wrote:

> Humor helps to combat my own grief and helps me accelerate the grief process for others . . . Humor is not something to be used to make fun of a situation, only to make fun out of what seems to be a hopeless catastrophe. Folks need something that will help get them through the times when nothing seems to calm them, not even reminders of comfort from the Bible given by well-meaning Christian friends. It's not that these scriptures aren't true; it's just that the pain is so intense you can't appreciate what the words are saying right at that moment. Later these scripture verses can

> become very meaningful, but, ironically, there were times during my own sieges of grief that the following observation made a kind of crazy sense to me: "Man cannot live by bread alone; he needs peanut butter, too."[5]

Laughing helps restore our joy and heads us toward a more positive emotional attitude. Even the silliest of comments can turn your tickle box upside down. One afternoon we were at the dry-cleaners, picking up my friend Laura's dress. It was one she had specially chosen to wear to the funeral of our beloved writing mentor, Jamie Buckingham. When she walked back to the car with a beautiful aqua blue dress, her husband said, "What, no black dress for the funeral?"

"No. Jamie would *die* if I wore black," she shot back.

"Jamie *is* dead, Laura," I said.

We broke out into sidesplitting laughter. Our pastor friend Jamie had such a wonderful sense of humor that we could just imagine him leaning over the balcony of heaven, laughing with us.

Whenever I drive my friend to her husband's gravesite, we walk a few feet further into the cemetery to get our chuckle for the day. Chiseled on the headstone of one husband and wife are these words: "We Had Fun." Can't you just imagine what their marriage was like?

Bill, a friend who brought laughter into our lives, had complicated medical conditions for years before he finally passed away. Because he was such a comic, his grown children saw that his obituary in the newspaper reflected humor too. It began with, *"Billy loved vanilla ice cream,"* and ended with *"in lieu of flowers, please send fried chicken."* Those of us who knew him well just roared with laughter. We Southerners understand that whenever there is a crowd to feed, fried chicken is bound to be on the menu. Billy's funeral drew a crowd, and folks stayed afterward to chew and chat. He would have loved it.

Let's look for more opportunities to let laughter lighten our days. Watch a funny movie or DVD. Go for a ride and look for comical signs or billboards. Call or visit a fun friend who makes you laugh at every crazy thing she says. Find moments in your day to remember something funny from your past. Laugh at yourself from time to time, at something simply ridiculous that you did.

Scripture

A merry heart does good, like medicine. (Proverbs 17:22)

Prayer

Lord, help me to learn to laugh again, and to turn my mourning into joy. Amen.

56.

Exchanging the Oil of Joy for Mourning

The Bible has more than 170 references that include the words laugh, laughter, or joy. God Himself laughs at His enemy (see Psalm 2:4). When the Israeli people were returning from captivity, they knew laughter, joy, and singing, because the Lord had done great things for them.

> Our mouths were filled with laughter,
> our tongues with songs of joy.
> Then it was said among the nations,
> "The Lord has done great things for them."
> The Lord has done great things for us,
> and we are filled with joy. (Psalm 126:2-3 NIV)

Perhaps it is hard to believe a day will come when your mouth will be filled with laughter, but it will. Let God Himself console you, replacing your mourning and spirit of heaviness for joy as this Scripture says:

> To console those who mourn in Zion,
> To give them beauty for ashes,

> The oil of joy for mourning,
> The garment of praise for the spirit of heaviness;
> That they may be called trees of righteousness,
> The planting of the Lord, that He may be glorified. (Isaiah 61:3)

One widow wondered if she would ever laugh again. "I was surprised by the thought, realizing I had always taken for granted the God-given blessing of laughter," she said. "I had cried so much after Bob's death. I knew God created tears for the purpose of healing my once-heavy and totally broken heart—but laughter? Then several of my former classmates invited me to go back to their state for a short visit, and while there they did so many extra special things that caused me to burst out laughing. I will forever treasure them for those moments. Now laughter comes more naturally once again."

Laughter offers a host of health benefits, including stress reduction. One university study showed that while mental stress has been linked to narrowing of blood vessels, laughter increases blood flow through relaxation of blood vessels.[6] Researchers can't say exactly how laughter benefits our heart. It could come from vigorous movement of the diaphragm muscles when we chuckle. Or laughter might trigger the release in the brain of endorphin hormones that have an effect on arteries. Whatever the reason, studies show laughter is good for the vascular system. Some doctors recommend you try to laugh fifteen minutes a day (but perhaps not continuously)!

That stretches it for me, but is a good goal. Liz is my long-distance fun friend I call whenever I need a chuckle, because she always makes me laugh. Do you have someone like that in your life? I hope so.

Scripture

And the ransomed of the Lord shall return, and come to Zion with singing, with everlasting joy on their heads. They shall obtain joy and gladness, and sorrow and sighing shall flee away. (Isaiah 35:10)

Prayer

Lord, when I reflect on the extraordinary and marvelous ways You have been with me, I have many reasons to rejoice. So now I praise You for my many happy times. Thank You for Your divine exchange: to give me joy instead of sorrow. Bring some joyful people into my life who will help me laugh more often. Amen.

57.

Laugh At Yourself

Can you laugh at yourself? You should try—it's helpful and it represents a step forward on your journey back to joyful living.

When I think back at some of the stupid things I did, I now can laugh. Here's one from my own journal, soon after my husband's death:

> The toilet is about to overflow and it is Sunday morning. How could he leave me in this mess? He always unstopped it and did not teach me how to use a plunger. I don't know the name of a plumber to call either. So I go to my computer, find the SEARCH button and type in "solutions to unstop toilet." Here come illustrations which I print out, in full color. I set them beside the toilet as I read and plunge, read and plunge. I try every method suggested—all three pages of instructions. I make numerous attempts. Nothing works. I pray under my breath for what seems like forever. I even find and fix a little part in the toilet tank.
>
> Finally, the toilet flushes. I actually shout, "Victory!" Of course, now the bathroom floor must be mopped and disinfected. But I did it! Praise God. Never did make it to church

this morning. But I learned that God and me and the Internet make a pretty good team. I still have those instructions in a bathroom drawer in case there is a next time.

You may wonder how I could have been so ill equipped. I was married to an aeronautical engineer who worked on spacecraft, and after retirement built houses. I did not have to learn about *anything* mechanical inside or outside the house. He fixed it all, including our cars.

Soon after I was widowed, I drove my friend Fran to a large wooded park. Here we were, two widows planning to enjoy the mild winter day by sitting on a bench at the far backside of the park, overlooking the beautiful bayou waters. The birds were comical as they swooped down to grab fish, sometimes fighting each other for their catch.

I looked at my friend who had her walking cane at her feet. Both of us were wearing black whistles around our neck. We had been told widows should keep a whistle to blow for help in case of danger. Suddenly, I started laughing.

"Fran, do you realize there is not another person around, not even a park ranger. So if any robber popped out of these woods behind us, there would not be anyone to hear our whistle blows for help. We are a helpless-looking couple of senior citizens."

She laughed. I laughed some more. We giggled and giggled, talking about all kinds of scenarios.

If you haven't laughed at yourself or some mess you found yourself in, maybe now is the time. God gave you a sense of humor as an ally and antidote. Use it often.

Scripture

Blessed are you who weep now, for you shall laugh. (Luke 6:21)

Prayer

Thank You, Lord, for showing me everyday things that can prompt me to laugh. I do want to laugh more often. Amen.

58.

Let's Laugh

I've discovered that when you live alone, you can get so self-centered you have to laugh at yourself now and again. I memorized the silly little poem below when I was five and playing house with my dolls. Now that I am a widow, I pull it out of my memory bank every once in a while. It keeps me from taking myself so seriously and reminds me that my world cannot just revolve around Me, Myself, and I. Perhaps it will give you a laugh as well.

My Tea Party

I had a little tea party
This afternoon at three.
It was very small
Three guests in all
I, Myself, and Me.
Myself ate up all the sandwiches
While I drank up the tea
It was also I
Who ate the pie
And passed the cake
To Me. (Author unknown)

Let's guard ourselves from carrying a "chip on our shoulder" because we are alone now, and instead find things to laugh about in our new lifestyle.

Scripture

Now may the God of hope fill you with all joy and peace in believing, that you may abound in hope by the power of the Holy Spirit.
(Romans 15:13)

Prayer

Lord, I am so thankful that You gave me a tickle box so I can laugh. Keep me from being so self-centered that I forget about others in my life. Show me ways that I can help bring them joy and laughter. Amen.

59. Restored to Life

Talk about restoration. Here is an illustration that tells it all . . .

In the book of Acts, there is a story of a widow named Tabitha, or Dorcas, a seamstress who made things for the poor. Because of her deeds of kindness, she was well known in the Christian circles of Joppa, located on the Mediterranean Sea about thirty-five miles northwest of Jerusalem. She was also known as a disciple of the Lord (see Acts 9:36–43).

One day she fell sick and died. The other women washed her body and laid it in an upper room. The Christians heard how a man named Aeneas had been paralyzed and bedridden for eight years, but was healed when the apostle Peter prayed for him. When they learned Peter was in a nearby village, they sent two men to get him to come pray for Dorcas.

As soon as Peter arrived they took him into the upper room and all the widows stood beside him weeping, showing him all the robes and other clothing that Tabitha made when she was with them.

Peter sent them out, got down on his knees, and prayed. Turning then to the dead woman he said, "Tabitha, arise." She opened her eyes, and when she saw Peter, she sat up. He took her by the hand and helped her to her feet. Then calling the believers, He presented her alive. The miracle became known all over Joppa and many believed in the Lord because of it.

Can you just picture the other widows gathered around this friend who had been restored to life? I ask myself questions. Were the other widows all seamstresses? Was this a sewing circle, or did they have varied talents they used in other ways? I picture how others would be blessed because Tabitha again was sewing for the poor and needy.

Some of us have felt dead inside for so long that we have let our dreams and talents die too. My "take away lesson" from Tabitha's resurrection is that today we can begin to allow God to restore our dashed hopes, dreams, and talents. He can send others into our lives as encouragers—to pray with us, and support us. But He can also give us a new lease on life—resurrecting the gifts we have within us so we too can use our talents to bless others.

Scripture

And the God of all grace, who called you to his eternal glory in Christ, after you have suffered a little while, will Himself restore you and make you strong, firm and steadfast. To Him be the power forever and ever. Amen. (1 Peter 5:10-11 NIV)

Prayer

I pray, God, that You will restore what it is in my life that I have let die. Stir up my gifts, dreams, and talents so I can be a blessing to those You bring into my path. After all, You are the Creator and You put those gifts in me. Amen.

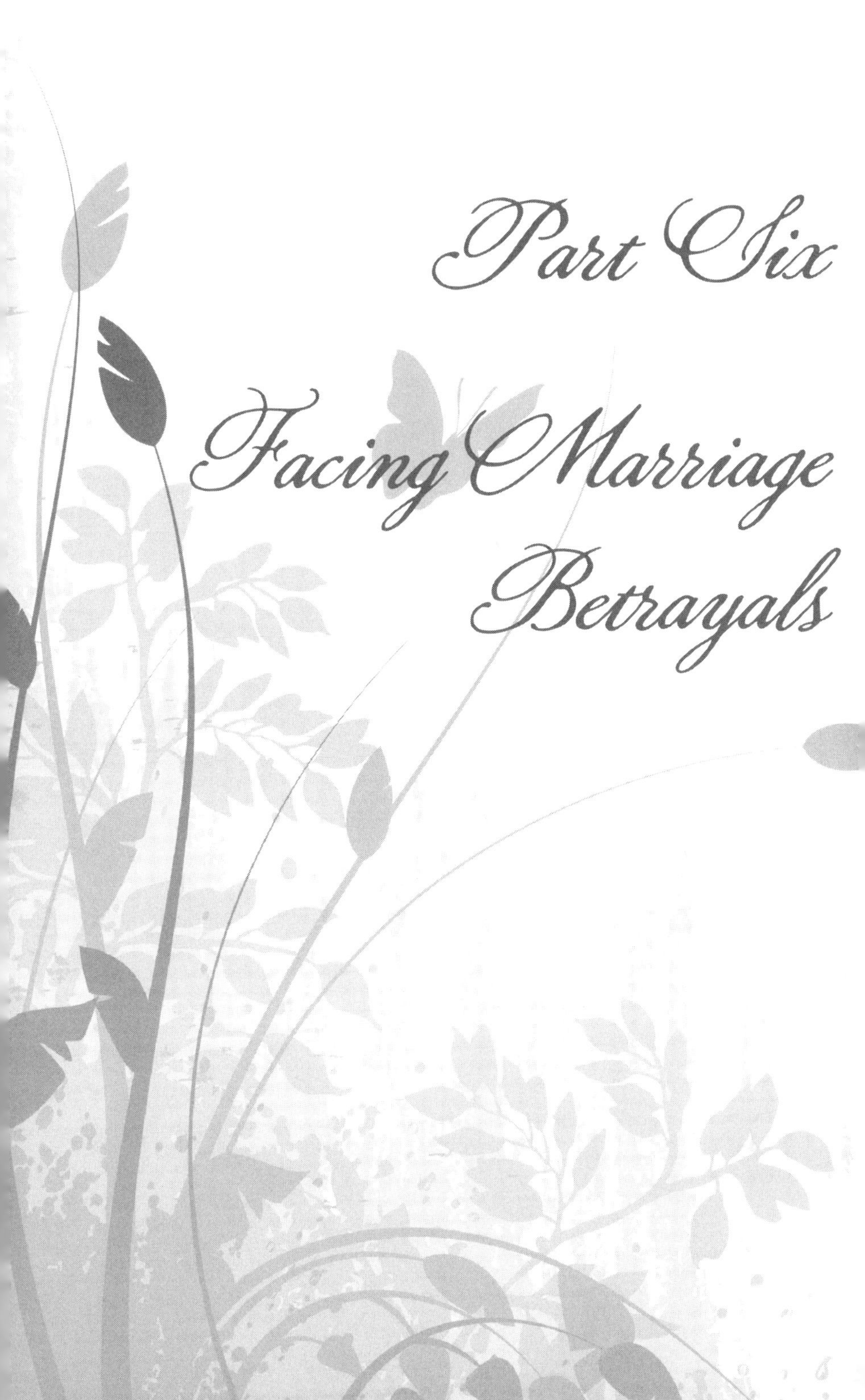

Part Six

Facing Marriage Betrayals

60.

The Aftermath of Betrayal

How does a woman handle widowhood when her married life was a sham? At her wedding, she stood before God and witnesses and took vows to honor this man she pledged her life to love. But somewhere along the way, he betrayed her. Maybe he had an affair. Perhaps he physically abused her. Or he might have been verbally and emotionally abusive. Maybe he withheld finances from her, or controlled her behavior in other manipulative ways.

Trena lived with an abusive husband for twenty-five years. He would demean her, accuse her of having affairs, and scream foul names at her. Even her best friend did not know how bad things were at home. Trena and her husband looked like a perfectly happy, successful, churchgoing, country-club couple. Like many women in similar situations, she stayed in the marriage for the sake of her children.

Then when her husband was in his early sixties, he died suddenly from a heart attack. After the funeral, Trena discovered hidden bottles of liquor and pornographic materials, evidence of just how bad his bondage had been. She even learned he'd had an affair with one of her friends, the very thing he had accused her of doing.

Whenever she recalled the obscene words he had called her, she trembled. She had to continually repeat Scriptures that affirmed who she was in God's sight; she fought to restore her true identity—at least in her own eyes. She said when you are falsely accused, you begin to believe the lies, and feel unclean. Finally, she was able to accept herself as loved by her one and only Master, the Lord. She has been a widow several years now, and is one of the most dedicated Christians I know.

Maybe you too suffered from mistreatment during your marriage. Let God love you through His Word as Trena did.

You may also want to ask Him to take away the painful memories and renew your mind. One widow wrote down all the wrongs committed against her on several sheets of paper, then one evening standing in her backyard, offered them to God, telling Him she forgave those wrongs and those who committed them, and burned her list in the barbeque grill.

Scripture

The Lord your God in your midst, The Mighty One, will save; He will rejoice over you with gladness, He will quiet you with His love, He will rejoice over you with singing. I will gather those who sorrow over the appointed assembly, who are among you, to whom its reproach is a burden. Behold, at that time I will deal with all who afflict you." (Zephaniah 3:17-19)

Prayer

Lord, I am so grateful that You took care of me through my days of mistreatment and unhappiness. Thank You too for the way You love and cherish me. I want to live the remainder of my days as You direct. May I always find happiness and fulfillment in You. Amen.

61.

Sadly, multitudes of women suffer mistreatment at the hands of their husbands. And yes, sadly many of these husbands are Christian men. A marriage counselor told me, "'Thou shall not kill' is one of the Ten Commandments, but many men are guilty of killing their wife's soul—her mind, will, emotions, and even her human spirit—with sharp, hateful, accusing barbs. Words are powerful and they can be very harmful."

Susan stayed in an abusive marriage forty-eight years because she did not want her children to grow up in a one-parent home, as she had. She'd hoped that her behavior would win her husband to the Lord, as she read in 1 Peter 3:1. But unfortunately he became an alcoholic, smoked heavily, and had several affairs. His abusive name-calling and cursing sometimes led to violent behavior, and two times she had to call the police.

Finances were always an issue. When she was involved in a fender bender, he demanded she come up with the $1,000 deductible required to repair the car. She only had $200 in the bank but somehow it multiplied to the needed amount, though no deposits were made, so she called it her "God miracle."

When I heard her story, I thought of the widow in the Old Testament who was in dire need of provision for herself and her sons, and all they had was a jar of oil. The prophet Elisha instructed her to borrow lots of vessels and to pour her little bit of oil into them. The oil multiplied until all the vessels were filled. Then she was able to sell the oil, pay her debts, and live on the rest (see 2 Kings 4:1-7). Susan told me God came through for her during her abusive marriage, and later when she became a widow. And He can for *anyone* who cries out to Him!

As her husband was dying of heart congestion, Susan did her best to care for him. "I lived with the motto of not returning evil with evil, but with good," she said. "For years I had shed tears over him. Yes, I was disappointed that my marriage had not turned out as I envisioned. Even as I walked through my own trial of cancer, I kept on praying and serving him. For years I attended meetings for spouses of alcoholics. Just once I wanted to hear him say he was sorry for how he treated me, but he never did. Truthfully, I did not shed a tear when he died. I had tried to walk in forgiveness. I loved the Lord and did whatever He instructed me to do in caring for a sick alcoholic."

Susan and Trena and countless other women whose marriages were marred by ill treatment can be reminded of how our Creator God sees them.

You are precious in His sight. You have value. You were created in the image of God. You did not deserve to be treated as a "thing." If you haven't already, tell the Lord about each hurt and ask for His healing touch. To complete your healing, you may need to seek help from a Christian counselor. Take one step at a time, trusting the Lord to bring you to victory over the painful memories and wounds.

Scripture

I will praise You, for I am fearfully and wonderfully made; marvelous are Your works . . . Your eyes saw my substance, being yet unformed. And in Your book they all were written, the days fashioned for me . . . How precious also are Your thoughts to me, O God! How great the sum of them. If I should count them, they would be more in number than the sand; When I awake, I am still with You."

(Psalm 139:14, 16-18)

Prayer

Lord, I know You love me with an everlasting love. I give You the horrible memories that still haunt me; I believe You are restoring my whole being. I choose to move in forgiveness and let go of the past. Thank You for the opportunity I have to live and enjoy this beautiful world. Thank You that Jesus came to give me hope and eternal life. Amen.

62.

What If We Divorced?

Can a divorcée be considered a widow? Not technically. But some refer to themselves as "Grass Widows," when their husbands die after their divorce.

One told me, "No one knows how upset you feel when your ex-husband dies, and you can't even explain it because you are considered a divorcée, not a widow. But he fathered my two children, and I still cared for him. He left me for a younger woman and cut himself off from the kids. My daughter had not seen him in twenty years. But when he was on his deathbed, I called our children to come see him and they were glad they did. I told my son as he sobbed after the burial that I never quit caring for his dad. I hated what he did to us, deserting us, but I did not hate him. It had taken me five years to get over my bitterness of his betrayal, and his failure to support us financially after he left. No, I did not go to the funeral, but I grieved at home and no one ever asked how I felt."

Another divorced friend did go to her ex-husband's private graveside service for the sake of their grown children. They had been married a long time but divorced when he did not bring his lust for other women under control. At his death, she grieved over him and for her children who loved him, because he was their dad.

If you feel the need to grieve when your former husband dies, go ahead! Something deep down inside you may need to be expressed. Maybe you are over your anger, but maybe you are not. Maybe you are still hurt to the quick, and need to express it in words to a trusted friend, or in private talks with God. Don't be like the widow who stuffed her hurt so deep down, no one suspected she needed healing. She finally talked to me and we prayed together.

Scripture

So I will restore to you the years that the swarming locust has eaten . . . I am the Lord Your God and there is no other. My people shall never be put to shame. (Joel 2:25, 27)

Prayer

Lord, I am sorry my marriage shattered. Please remove from me feelings of betrayal, shame, resentment, and loneliness. Put a hedge around my mind and heart so I will not fall back into anger or bitterness. Restore my life and help me to know my true worth and significance. God, You are the key to my future. I ask You to protect me physically, financially, emotionally, and in every way I need it. Amen.

Children Suffer Too

Suicide—it is one of the most heartbreaking and tragic acts a person can commit.

When a husband of twenty years makes his wife a widow by his own rash choice, how does she deal with the mess that ensues? Sadly, while researching this book, I talked to several women who have experienced such circumstances. All had children. Their husbands were Christians, but mental illness took its toll. So these widows were left to pick up the pieces, comfort the children, and make critical decisions they had never faced before. Here's just one story . . .

Imagine the heartache Mindy felt when the man she had loved since she was a fifteen-year-old girl took his life. Though he was on anti-depression medications, Mindy's forty-six-year-old husband committed suicide while out of town. She was left to deal with the grief, shame, and upheaval—in addition to trying to comfort their five children, all under age thirteen. At first, Mindy was in shock; then she was angry. One minor bright spot: Because she home-schooled the children, she was glad they didn't have to interact with other children at school so soon after this tragedy.

Mindy's oldest, a thirteen-year-old son, was probably affected the most and refused to return to their rental house after it happened. It was too full of memories of scary things his depressed dad had done. So Mindy moved the family into another rental. She felt she couldn't cry in front of the kids, so she took bicycle rides to talk to the Lord and cry her heart out.

"Right after his death, I would look down the street as though expecting him to walk back to me," she recalled. "When I accepted that his death was real and he was not coming home, I leaned further into the arms of the Lord. I had read the Scripture in Isaiah 54 where it says the Lord my Maker is my Husband. So I started treating Father God as my husband. If I couldn't fix a bicycle, I'd ask Him how, and the directions would come clearly to me. If the garage door didn't work, I'd read the manual that came with it to see how to repair it. The Lord impressed upon me that the Bible is also my 'manual' for my life, and for raising my children. I already knew that, but the Bible became so much more precious to me as I read it and pressed closer to the Lord."

Despite her progress, "One day while crying on my bike ride, I asked God why my husband died. He gave me a strange Scripture, which I have since read many times in the Amplified version. Other people might not understand it, and so it was possibly only a passage for me." But here it is:

> The righteous man perishes, and no one lays it to heart; and merciful and devout men are taken away, with no one considering that the uncompromisingly upright and godly person is taken away from the calamity and evil to come [even through wickedness]. He [in death] enters into peace; they rest in their beds, each one who walks straight and in his uprightness (Isaiah 57:1-2 AMP).

Mindy felt the Lord was telling her that her late husband was taken away from calamity and evil to come, and to enter peace and rest. He had not been at rest for months and had been in hospitals, therapy, and on medications. Yes, he was a believer, but mental illness got the best of him. Since he had been exhibiting erratic behavior before his death, she felt that the Lord protected her and the children, since some suicidal parents take the lives of their family also.

He had been a good dad in providing financially, and had faithfully paid for life insurance for years. So after his death, Mindy had the funds to make a down payment on a house, trade in his truck for a car, and do other things to help make life for the children more stable.

But of course, it did not take away her heartbreak. Her daughter wanted to look at family videos often because they had scenes with her dad. But one son did not want to see videos and, in fact, wanted all the pictures of their dad removed from the house. Once during a time of anger, she herself sent his pictures flying across the room like Frisbees.

Her church friends were comforting, especially the Widows Home Group, where the older widows encouraged her each month. She still home-schools the children and lives as best she can. It has been five years and, yes, she has learned she can do lots of things she never imagined.

The ache in her heart is still there for the man she had loved since high school. Yet now God is her Husband, and she consults Him about all her decisions.

As you read her story, maybe you didn't know how to react. But here is something she said: "In general, church people do not know how to respond to a tragedy like this—what to say, what to do for the family. Please be considerate, understanding, and show the compassion of the Lord to a family walking through such heartache. And do not judge the husband, because you do not know all the torment he went through."

Scripture

Now may the God of patience and comfort grant you to be like-minded toward one another, according to Christ Jesus. (Romans 15:5)

Prayer

Lord, I thank You that You are my husband now. I depend on You entirely for all my life decisions. Help my children to remember good things about their dad. Heal their hearts and minds and keep them from being permanently crippled by his wrong choice. I pray that they will fulfill their destiny and become godly adults who will love and serve You and contribute their talents to make this a better world. I ask in Jesus' name. Amen.

64.

Suicide Touches Many Facets of Life

Here's the story of a wife who spells out some of the heartache she suffered both before and after her husband's death from suicide. She wrote:

> The suicide of a loved one comes with its own set of issues. It is like a sea creature with many tentacles, touching on many facets of life. My husband suffered from Bipolar Disorder for more than twelve years. We somehow managed to get through five mental breakdowns, two suicide interventions, and numerous manic phases before he finally took his own life. I was preparing for a third intervention, having just learned that he had secretly taken himself off all his medications.
>
> He had become increasingly agitated and began carrying a loaded gun in his pocket every day. I was terribly concerned for myself, my children, and my little grandchildren who often visited us. I became more and more withdrawn, crying privately as I interceded on my husband's behalf, and for my own as well.
>
> Things were rapidly falling apart in our lives. We had lost several businesses due to internal problems, and the recession.

We struggled to earn enough income to keep us going, but were unable to find suitable work. We were about to lose our home. I could see my husband quickly losing control.

One day I felt the Lord warn me that something difficult was ahead, but He said, "Do not fear, for I will walk with you every step along the way. I won't ever leave you, nor forsake you. Take my hand, and trust Me." I fasted, prayed, and sought professional help. I finally had to admit that I hadn't learned to properly cope with my husband's mental illness. I hadn't set healthy boundaries. My counselor told me to first keep myself safe, and then confront him about his illness.

I tried to reason with him that the sickness was not his fault, and that he had to be the one to take responsibility. He had to allow me to remove all weapons from the home; he had to get back on his medicine and get professional counseling for our safety and well-being. I made him promise me that no matter what, he wouldn't hurt himself. I begged him to think of our children and how much it would hurt them if he harmed himself. He assured me he wanted to live, and I believed him.

Three days later, he killed himself. My son found him when he returned from work that evening. How I wish it had been me who found him instead of my son! He has suffered greatly because of it. My children were shocked and horrified. My young grandchildren couldn't understand why their grandpa had gone to heaven. People from everywhere came to console us. Over two thousand people attended his service. He was a bright, energetic, generous, and loving man. He loved people, and he was loved in return. Few knew of the dark side he had tried so hard to conceal. I, too, had covered for him.

A traumatic death causes everyone to look for answers. I also discovered that it causes many to seek something or someone to blame. I became the one to blame. I not only had to deal with the grief of losing my husband, whom I dearly loved, but I had to cope with the harsh judging of my actions from those I thought were my friends and loving family members.

To make matters worse, I was in a mess financially. I did receive the proceeds from insurance, but unfortunately, our debt was nearly equal to what I received. I didn't know how I was going to get everything straightened out. My poor husband must have thought that the only way he could help us financially was to take his life so I could use the monies to help get us out of trouble. I had to navigate through rough, shark-infested waters. It took me a year to negotiate a short sale on my house. I saw God walk me through this valley of death.

The loneliness I felt after my husband died was almost unbearable at times. I had hoped that family members and friends would reach out on a regular basis, just to keep up with me, but calls became few and far between.

Did I miss and grieve for my husband? Most definitely! But he chose to end his life, to leave our children and me. I wrote him a letter a year after his death. There is much I would want him to know, and I sometimes wonder if the Lord sits down and explains those things to our loved ones when they reach the other side.

Today I am very happily married to a man who is strong in faith, a man of prayer, and for whom I thank God.

This woman moved with her new husband to a different city to start over. Since her grown children were not happy that she remarried, their estrangement has caused her heartache. But she is glad she is not living alone now, and expects a happy reconciliation someday.

I included her story here for us to better understand what widows of suicide victims go through. I hope it encourages us to reach out to the widow who is facing the embarrassment, loneliness, and financial consequences she must endure because of her husband's choice of death. May God comfort all of us who have been through the sadness of burying our spouses.

Scripture

Blessed be the God and Father of our Lord Jesus Christ, the Father of mercies and God of all comfort, who comforts us in all our tribulation, that we may be able to comfort those who are in any trouble, with the comfort with which we ourselves are comforted by God.
(2 Corinthians 1:3-4)

Prayer

Thank You, Lord, for taking care of all the details for me after I became a widow through tragic circumstances. Please help restore my relationships with those I love most dearly. Come in Your power and unite what is now divided. I thank You in advance because I know You are the Restorer of broken hearts. Amen.

65.

Jesus Understands Betrayal

No one understands betrayal more than Jesus, who was betrayed by one of His inner circle of disciples; Judas sold Him out for a kiss and thirty pieces of silver. When Judas learned that because of his act Jesus was condemned to die, he was remorseful. He attempted to return the silver to the chief priests and elders—the religious ones—who demanded Jesus' death, but they didn't want it back. Judas threw down the silver and went and hanged himself (see Matthew 26:47-48; Matthew 27:3-5).

Jesus suffered severe beatings and the agony of death on the cross. But the tomb could not hold Him and He arose, going to heaven where He sits as our Intercessor, and soon coming King.

Hallelujah, He arose!

Scripture

Even my own familiar friend in whom I trusted, who ate my bread, has lifted up his heel against me. But You, O Lord, be merciful to me, and raise me up. (Psalm 41:9-10)

Prayer

Lord, I am so glad that when I experience betrayal, You comfort me. Thank You for enduring the pain of the cross for me. I choose to forgive those who have mistreated me, just as You forgave me for my sins. Amen.

Part Seven

Agreeing with God and Prayer Partners

66.

Praying the Alphabet, Worshipping God

Standing at this critical crossroads in our lives, uncertain what tomorrow may bring, we can make our today and tomorrows go more smoothly by worshipping our Lord and agreeing with His written Word.

With the living creatures in heaven, we can say, "You are worthy, O Lord, to receive glory and honor and power; for You created all things, and by Your will they exist and were created" (Revelation 4:11).

Often during the time I set aside for prayer, I pray through the alphabet, concentrating on the characteristics of the Trinity—Our Heavenly Father's greatness; Jesus, His Son's love to die for our sins; and the Holy Spirit, our Comforter and Teacher. Then I add my praise and thanks aloud, naming things about whom the Godhead is, and why I am grateful. You can add others to this list:

A: Almighty God, Abba Father, Ancient of Days, Awesome God, Alpha and Omega

B: Bread of Life, Bright and Morning Star, Balm of Gilead, Beginning and the End, Blood of the Lamb, Blessing and Honor and Glory and Power are due Your Name

C: Christ, Covenant Keeper, Comforter

D: Divine, Deliverer, Destroyer of Sin

E: Eternal, Everlasting God, Excellent, Exalted, Encourager

F: Father, Faithful Friend, Forgiver, Faultless, Fortress

G: Good Shepherd, God of Glory, Grace, Giver of Life

H: Holy One, Holy Spirit, High Priest, Healer, Helper, Hope

I: Immanuel, I AM, Indescribable, Immortal, Invisible

J: Jehovah, Jesus, Just Judge

K: King of Kings, Keeper, Kind, Knowing

L: Lord of Lords, Lamb of God, Lord God Almighty, Living Word, Light of the World, Lord of Hosts, Lion of Judah

M: Master, Maker of Heaven and Earth, Messiah, Mediator, Magnificent, Majestic

N: Name Above All Names, Nazarene, New Mercies Every Morning

O: Omnipotent, Omnipresent, Only Begotten, Omega

P: Prince of Peace, Provider, Potter, Protector, Praiseworthy

Q: Quieter of My Storms, Quite a Provider, Quencher of My Thirst

R: Redeemer, Righteous, Repairer of the Breach, Restorer, Rock of Salvation

S: Savior, Shepherd, Son of God, Son of Man

T: Truth, Teacher, Transformer, Trustworthy, Triumphant

U: Understanding, Universal, Upright

V: Victorious, Vine, Virtuous, Voice of God

W: Warrior, Worthy, Wise, Who Is and Who Was and Who Is to Come, The Word

X: eXtra-ordinary in All Your Ways

Y: Yahweh (Hebrew name for God, Jehovah), Yoke

Z: Zealous—He will arouse His zeal like a man of war. He will prevail against His enemies (see Isaiah 42:13 NASB).

Scripture

Enter into His gates with thanksgiving, and into His courts with praise. Be thankful to Him and bless His name. For the Lord is good; His mercy is everlasting, and His truth endures to all generations.
(Psalm 100:4-5)

Prayer

Thank You, Lord, that I can exalt You in so many ways; so many words describe Your character and Your loving-kindness. Accept my praise and worship of You. Amen.

67.

Personalizing Scripture

As mentioned earlier, personalizing Scripture helps you express what you feel deep down. Here is one example, based on Deuteronomy 7:9:

> Lord, You are a faithful God who keeps covenant and mercy for a thousand generations with those who love You and keep your commandments. Lord, I stand in amazement that I can be in covenant with You, the Creator of the universe. Thank You that You watch over me and move in my behalf. I trust You today to do that with (name personal concerns).

During petition prayers, I daily ask for *God's presence, protection, provision, and for His precious promises to be fulfilled in my life* (and my family's). Why pray? Jesus said, "Ask, and it will be given to you; seek, and you will find; knock, and it will be opened to you" (Matthew 7:7). Another Scripture we've already mentioned says, "For all the promises of God in Him are Yes, and in Him Amen, to the glory of God through us" (2 Corinthians 1:20). God wants us to partner with Him.

Jack Hayford writes concerning this:

> God wills that we partner with Him in seeing His promises fulfilled. Most promises are not automatically fulfilled apart from prayerful, humble request. He can keep His promises, He wills to keep His promises, but He wants us to pray . . . It is by this partnership in prayer that a believer may fulfill Jesus' instruction to pray, "Thy will be done in earth, as it is in heaven." The target of our fellowship with Him is to lead us into partnership with Him.[1]

In Luke 18, Jesus tells a parable to admonish His followers to pray and not lose heart. A widow comes to a city judge who does not fear God or man, meaning he probably has no personal interest in the needs of the Jewish people. But this widow keeps coming to his courtroom, asking justice for herself, or to be avenged. But the judge will not act. However, the widow's persistence wears down his reluctance.

Jesus ends this parable: "Then the Lord said, 'Listen to what the unjust judge says! And will not [our just] God defend and protect and avenge His elect (His chosen ones), who cry to Him day and night? Will He defer them and delay help on their behalf? I tell you, He will defend and protect and avenge them speedily. However, when the Son of Man comes, will He find [persistence in] faith on the earth?'" (Luke 18:6-8 AMP).

God is not like the unjust judge who had to be badgered until he grew weary and gave in.[2] He wants us to come to Him in faith with bold, persistent prayers and without hesitancy. He is always available to hear our petitions. And don't worry if you sound like a broken record. He loves to hear from you, His daughter! Just talk to Him. And talk some more.

Scripture

Our Father in heaven, Hallowed be Your name. Your kingdom come, Your will be done on earth as it is in heaven . . . For Yours is the kingdom and the power and the glory forever. Amen.
(Matthew 6:9-10, 13)

Prayer

Lord, thank You that I can come boldly to You without hesitation, knowing that You long to hear my prayer, and to fellowship with me. What a privilege! Thank You, Father God. Amen.

68.

Enlisting a Prayer Team

Not only do we want to partner with God, but having a prayer partner or prayer support team is a powerful source of strength. Jesus Himself said, "I say to you that if two of you agree on earth concerning anything that they ask, it will be done for them by My Father in heaven. For where two or three are gathered together in My name, I am there in the midst of them" (Matthew 18:19, 20). To *agree* here means to pray together in harmony much like a symphony orchestra.

When the 120 believers were in the Upper Room waiting for the outpouring of the Holy Spirit "they continued with one accord in prayer and supplication . . . and when the day of Pentecost was fully come, they were all with one accord in one place" (Acts 1:14; 2:1 KJV). The word accord here means "being in agreement, having group unity, having one mind and purpose."[3]

For years, my faithful prayer partner, Tommie, and I prayed almost every day via phone. She was with me when my husband made his exit to heaven, and I could call her day or night. She would quote just the Scripture I needed that day, and then pray specifically for my concern. Then a few months ago, she too left for heaven. So many times I have picked up the phone to ask her to pray, forgetting she no longer lives across the three-mile bridge from me. Her absence has left such a void in my life.

Thankfully, I have others who stand in the prayer gap with me, and some of us communicate via email and telephone. Having prayer partners is a two-way commitment because we pray for one another. When my children were young and we lived in another community, my friend, Lib, and I prayed on the phone specifically for our youngsters for five minutes every weekday for seventeen years. God answered many of our prayers of agreement. (See my book A *Mother's Guide to Praying for Your Children*).[4]

Recently, while at a church's Widows Support Group, I asked one of the youngest widows, a mother of five who is still in her 40s, how she felt about attending a gathering with so many older widows. "I get golden wisdom from these women who advise me and pray for me," she replied. "I won't miss this monthly meeting for anything." Unfortunately, too few churches have similar widows support groups. If yours does not, maybe one day you will want to help start one.

Scripture

Confess your trespasses to one another and pray for one another, that you may be healed. The effective fervent prayer of a righteous man [or woman] avails much. (James 5:16)

Prayer

Thank You for the faithful friends who have interceded for me; praying faithfully for me to emerge from my darkest hour, when my soul ached painfully. You know who they are so I ask for You to bless them, Lord. Amen.

69.

Letting Go and Trusting God

Sometimes God wants us to come to a newer place of trusting Him. The next story illustrates this . . .

Jackie and Jamie Buckingham had been married thirty-eight years when Jamie died from a recurring illness. Some months after his death, Jackie shared her struggles with me.

"When you are married, you become one. Then when your mate is gone, it seems as if half of you is gone. I felt like a part of me had been amputated," she admitted.

But then she told me how God and others—through their prayers—intervened to bring her hope. "It is God's grace and mercy that have kept me going," she said. "I could have pulled the covers over my head and been depressed. But I had to make a choice to believe that God has a purpose and plan for me even now. I'd wake up in the middle of the night praying the *Jesus Prayer*—'Jesus Christ, Son of God, have mercy on me!' And many times I've cried out, 'Lord, please put me on someone's heart to pray for me.' When I sense His peace come over me, I know someone, somewhere, has been praying."

Along the way, Jackie learned valuable lessons about relying on the Lord. "You don't realize Jesus is all you need until He is all you have," she added. "I've come to understand there is a difference between grieving and self-pity (the latter is sin). From time to time, I have to ask myself, '*Am I grieving over the fact that Jamie is gone? Or am I into self-pity?*' I constantly look to the Lord to help me stay focused on Him."[5]

At Jamie's memorial service, Jackie had stood with her five children and thirteen grandchildren on the church's platform and invited us all to participate in a celebration of his life. We did, with congregational singing, and then several in the audience told remembrances of ways he had touched their lives.

Jackie's prayer lessons could be put into a prayer like this: "Lord, help me to keep my focus on You, the One who comforts me! Keep me from self-pity. I thank You for being there for my children, my grandchildren, and me. Thank You for those who have prayed for me during my darkest hours. I praise You for Your sustaining love and protection. In the precious name of Jesus, I pray. Amen."

Dear sister in Christ, I know your new journey has not been easy. I hope that you have developed an even closer personal relationship with Jesus; that you have learned to trust Father God as your Husband and Provider; and that you have discovered that the Holy Spirit wants to be your Comforter and Teacher. Jesus promised that when He left this earth, He would ask the Father to send "another Helper, that He may abide with you forever" (John 14:16). That Helper is the Holy Spirit (see Luke 24:49; Acts 1:8; Romans 8: 26-27).

I pray that you will find a faithful prayer partner who will pray with you on a regular basis; one who will keep your requests confidential, and will be a godly influence and encourager to you. Maybe you will even find an entire prayer support team.

When the Lord told me to get up from my husband's gravesite and "act alive," believe me, those next months were not easy. Today, I want more than ever to act alive. And I believe you do too. So let's keep our eyes and ears focused on our God, who offers hope for any widow's heart!

Scripture

But as it is written: "Eye has not seen, nor ear heard, nor have entered into the heart of man [or woman] the things which God has prepared for those who love Him." (1 Corinthians 2:9)

Prayer

Lord, I desire to move into new levels of praise and worship of You. When I reflect on all You have already done for me, I am amazed and thankful. I know too that You have something greater for me than I can imagine. Now help me to finish the race You have for me to run, and may I do it well. I ask in Jesus' name. Amen.

70.

Living My Dash Well

Most gravestones have a dash between the birthday and the death of the person buried there. Linda Ellis wrote a famous poem called "The Dash." This inspiring piece challenges us to live our lives well between the dash—from our birth to our death. She asks: when our eulogy is being read, with our "life's actions to rehash," would we be proud of how we spent our dash?[6] Not far from my husband's grave is a monument marking the grave of a young woman, with the inscription, "She Lived Her Dash Well."

I was greatly impacted by "The Dash" when it first came out, and have since pondered its message many times. But today I am more interested in what God thinks about how I am living out my "dash years." I yearn to say with the apostle Paul, "I have fought the good fight, I have finished the race, I have kept the faith. Finally, there is laid up for me the crown of righteousness, which the Lord, the righteous Judge, will give to me on that Day, and not to me only but also to all who have loved His appearing" (2 Timothy 4:7-8).

Yes, as widows we are at critical crossroads, but we do have a choice: to stay in our grief or live victoriously with hope in our heart. I choose to let God impart that hope and guide me on this journey.

My husband's dash is finished. His race is run. My dash is still being lived out, my race still being run. I hope when mine is over that my headstone can read, "She Finished the Race Well."

Isn't that your desire too?

Scripture

Therefore we also, since we are surrounded by so great a cloud of witnesses, let us lay aside every weight, and the sin which so easily ensnares us, and let us run with endurance the race that is set before us, looking unto Jesus, the author and finisher of our faith.
(Hebrews 12:1-2)

Prayer

Lord, now help me to finish the race You have for me to run. May I do it in such a manner that You will be pleased. Amen.

Endnotes

Part One: Saying Goodbye

1. Doug Manning, *Don't Take My Grief Away from Me* (Oklahoma City, Okla.: In-Sight Books, 1979), p. 65.
2. Manning, *Don't Take My Grief Away from Me*, p. 65.
3. Adapted from: Quin Sherrer and Ruthanne Garlock, *Lord, Help Me Break This Habit* (Grand Rapids, Mich.: Chosen Books, 2009), p. 72.
4. Adapted from: Sherrer and Garlock, *Lord, Help Me Break This Habit*, p. 70.
5. James Strong, *Strong's Exhaustive Concordance of the Bible* (Grand Rapids, Mich.: Zondervan, 2001), #3089.
6. Dutch Sheets, *Becoming Who You Are* (Minneapolis, Minn.: Bethany House, 2007), p. 34.
7. Randy Alcorn, *Heaven* (Wheaton, Ill.: Tyndale House, 2004), p. 73.
8. Catherine Marshall, *To Live Again* (New York: Avon Books, 1972), pp. 14-15.
9. Manning, *Don't Take My Grief Away From Me*, pp. 120-121.
10. Wikipedia, "Queen Victoria," www:Wikipedia.org/wiki/Victoria_of_the_United Kingdom.
11. Strong, *The Strongest Strong's Exhaustive Concordance of the Bible* (Grand Rapids, Mich.: Zondervan, 2004), #2580 and #2603.
12. Jack W. Hayford, ed., *Spirit-Filled Life Bible* (Nashville, Tenn.: Thomas Nelson, 1991) notes on Ruth 4:22, p. 393. Also *Strong's #7725*.

Part Two: Transitioning from Here to There

1. U.S. Bureau of the Census (1999) as reported on website: www.widows-bridge.com/stats.asp.
2. *Vita Journal*, "Older Americans: a snapshot," Scottsdale, Ariz., March 2012, p. 12.
3. See: www.personalpromisebible.com, or call 866-968-7242.
4. "Tell Me the Story of Jesus," Fanny Crosby, published in 1880. Public domain.

Part Three: Dealing With Emotions

1. Genevieve Davis Ginsburg, *Widow to Widow* (Tucson, Ariz.: Fisher Books, 1995), p. 25.
2. Ginsburg, *Widow to Widow*, p. 25.
3. Merriam Webster Online Dictionary, "forgive." See also *James Strong, Strong's Exhaustive Concordance*, Biblesoft's PC Bible Study, 2007. Greek references on "forgive," #630, #863, #5483.
4. Corrie ten Boom with Jamie Buckingham, *Tramp for the Lord* (Grand Rapids, Mich.: Fleming Revell, 1974), pp. 179, 180.
5. Quin Sherrer and Ruthanne Garlock, *A Woman's Guide to Breaking Bondages* (Ann Arbor, Mich.: Servant Publication, 1994), pp. 190-192.
6. Sherrer and Garlock, *A Woman's Guide to Breaking Bondages*, p. 190.
7. Hannah Whitall Smith, *The God of All Comfort* (Chicago: Moody, 1956), p. 112.
8. Corrie ten Boom, *Clippings from My Notebook* (Nashville, Tenn.: Thomas Nelson, 1982), p. 33.
9. Hayford, *Spirit-Filled Life Bible*, p. 1415.
10. Fred Smith, "Wait to Worry," *The Christian Reader*, June 1993, p. 53.
11. Ginsburg, *Widow to Widow*, p. 32.
12. Gail McWilliams, *Christ for the Nations* magazine, August 2009, p. 7.
13. Article by Megan Grober on Elisabeth Elliot and Rachel Saint found on website www:thetravelingteam.org/node/110.

14. Elisabeth Elliot, *Love Has A Price Tag* (Ann Arbor, Mich.: Servant, 1979), p. 108.

Part Four: Embracing a New Season

1. Miriam Neff, *From One Widow to Another* (Chicago: Moody Press, 2009), p. 12.
2. Neil T. Anderson and Hal Baumchen, *Finding Hope Again* (Ventura, Calif.: Regal, 1999), p. 222.
3. Adapted from: Quin Sherrer, *Listen, God is Speaking to You* (Ann Arbor, Mich.: Servant Publication, 1999), p. 50.
4. Hayford, *Spirit-Filled Life Bible*, p. 1034.
5. Hayford, *Spirit-Filled Life Bible*, commentary on Proverbs 14:26, p. 902.
6. Ann Spangler and Jean E. Syswerda, *Women of the Bible* (Grand Rapids, Mich.: Zondervan, 1999), p. 389.

Part Five: Renewing Hope in My Heart

1. Adapted from: Dutch Sheets, *Tell Your Heart to Beat Again* (Ventura, Calif.: Regal Books, 2002), pp. 128-132. Used with permission of author, who holds the copyright.
2. Hayford, *Spirit Filled Life Bible*, commentary on Hosea 2:15, p. 1260. Also: Strong's # 8615.
3. Judy Reamer, *Feelings Women Rarely Share* (Springdale, Penn.: Whitaker, 1987), p. 51.
4. Quin Sherrer and Ruthanne Garlock, *Prayers Women Pray* (Ann Arbor, Mich.: Servant, 1998), p. 96.
5. Barbara Johnson, *Pack Up Your Gloomies in a Great Big Box, Then Sit on the Lid and Laugh!* (Dallas, Tex.: Word, 1993), p. 32.
6. "Pick Laughter, It's the Better Medicine," *Vita Journal* (Scottsdale, Ariz., April 2010) p. 12.

Part Seven: Agreeing With God and Prayer Partners

1. Jack Hayford, *Prayer, Spiritual Warfare, and the Ministry of Angels* (Nashville, Tenn.: Thomas Nelson, 1993), p. 98.
2. Kenneth Barker, ed., *The NIV Study Bible,* New International Version (Grand Rapids, Mich.: Zondervan, 1985). Study Notes on Luke 18:6-8, p. 1574.
3. Hayford, *Spirit-Filled Life Bible*, p. 1624. Also: Strong's #3661.
4. See my book, *A Mother's Guide to Praying for Your Children* (Ventura, Calif.: Regal Books, 2011).
5. Adapted from: *A Woman's Guide to Getting Through Tough Times*, Quin Sherrer and Ruthanne Garlock (Ann Arbor, Mich.: Servant Publications, 1998), pp. 110-11.
6. www.lindaellis.net/the dash.

Appendix A

What to Do Before "Death Do You Part"

"Until death do us part," you promised in your marriage vows. But what can you do before death parts you?

This advice is for the woman who is not yet a widow. Suggestions came from many widows who wished they had asked these questions before their husbands died. They may not apply to you at all, and some may sound redundant, but they are worth asking.

Why not have an honest discussion with your husband and write down his answers to these questions, some of which might apply to both of you. Ask:

- Do you have a cemetery plot? Where? Cremation or burial? Funeral home selected?
- Do both of you have a will? Where is it kept?
- Do you have a living will? Hospitals ask for them when you are admitted.
- Do you (wife) understand how to pay all the bills yourself? Checks? Can you access the computer? Do you know the password? Can you access the online banking accounts or other important information stored on the computer? Be sure you know all passwords!

- Are your bank accounts in both names so you have access to adequate funds should he be unable to sign checks, or if he dies? If your banking account is not jointly held, are you the designated beneficiary for this account?
- Where are important papers kept? If in a safe deposit box, do you both have access and a key? Do you have keys to other lock boxes?
- What does the insurance policy provide for the surviving spouse? Where is it?
- Do you (wife) know how much income you will have to live on after he is gone?
- Do you (wife) know whom to contact to get funds immediately? (Phone numbers and addresses.)
- Are the names of the beneficiaries on his policies up-to-date? For instance, if one of the beneficiaries preceded him in death, he may have forgotten to change the names on insurance policies, bank accounts, or retirement funds, causing a delay due to probate court.
- Does your spouse have you as his power of attorney, and an alternative? Consider this true scenario: The husband had dementia so badly he could not make decisions, so as power of attorney, his wife did all the legal paperwork. But she died unexpectedly and there was not an alternative power of attorney. Things were tied up in probate court.
- Does his will state how he wants your children to be provided for? Has he made it clear so you don't have a hassle with them later?
- About your (wife's) will: Does it cover your own wishes for your husband if you go first? Or your children?

- Is the car title also in your (wife's) name so you can sell or trade it in later?
- Where are the titles to the car, boat, camper, house, or other properties?
- If you are buying your home, is it also in your (wife's) name?
- What are his wishes about what to do with the house? Will he leave that decision up to you?
- If you (wife) will need to go to probate court, will you have enough immediate funds to tide you over?
- Do you (wife) know name/phone/address of: your husband's lawyer? CPA? Insurance agent? Social security office? Bank manager? Stockbroker? Go meet them before you need them.
- Do you (wife) know where the tax returns are from previous years?
- Do you know the contact information for employer benefits?
- While he is still living, apply for a credit card in your (wife's) name based on her credit rating/history—one that cannot be cancelled if he dies.
- Do you have all home accounts in both of your names so you won't have to switch them over later? If not, consider finding out how to do that. Some utility companies, however, will not allow but one name on a bill; others will put the bill in both names if the husband and wife go in at the same time and furnish required data.
- What are your wishes about terminal care? Talk openly and honestly about this.
- Is your husband willing to consider a nursing home if you (wife) cannot care for him alone?
- Do you have funds to cover someone helping with home care?

Invite Jesus into Your Life

If you do not know Jesus as your Savior and Lord, here is a prayer you can pray:

Lord Jesus, please reveal Yourself to me. I want to know You in a real and personal way. I admit I am a sinner. Please forgive me for walking in my own selfish ways. I believe You are the Son of God who came to earth, died on the cross, and shed Your blood for my sins. I believe You rose from the dead and are seated at the right hand of the Father in heaven. I thank You for forgiving me of my sins. I receive You as my Lord and Savior. I want to live my life to please You. Please send the Holy Spirit to strengthen and empower me. Thank You for the free gift of salvation that will enable me to live with You forever. Amen.

Appendix B

Recommended Books and Websites

Websites for Widows:

www.widowconnection.com

www.sisterhoodofwidows.com

www.widowsbridge.com

Recommended Books:

Jack Canfield and Mark Victor Hansen, *Chicken Soup for the Grieving Soul*, Health Communications (2003).

Carol W. Cornish, *The Undistracted Widow, Living for God After Losing Your Husband*, Crossway (2010).

Genevieve Davis Ginsburg, *Widow to Widow*, Fisher Books (1997).

Doug Manning, *Don't Take My Grief Away From Me*, In-Sight Books (1994).

Miriam Neff, *From One Widow to Another*, Moody Publishers (2009).

Lois Mowday Rabey, *When Your Soul Aches*, Waterbrook Press (2000).

Kathleen M. Rehl, *Moving Forward On Your Own: A Financial Guidebook for Widows*, Rehl Financial Advisors (2010).

Joyce Rogers, *Grace for a Widow—Journey Through the Fog*, B&H Publishers (2009).

Dutch Sheets, *Intercessory Prayer*, Regal Books (1996).

Dutch Sheets, *Tell Your Heart to Beat Again*, Regal Books (2002).

Dutch Sheets, *Dream: Discovering God's Purpose for Your Life*, Bethany House (2012).

Quin Sherrer, *A Mother's Guide to Praying for Your Children*, Regal Books (2011).

Quin Sherrer, Ruthanne Garlock, *Grandma, I Need Your Prayers*, Zondervan (2002).

Quin Sherrer, Ruthanne Garlock, *A Woman's Guide to Spiritual Warfare*, Regal Books (2010).

Quin Sherrer, Ruthanne Garlock, *The Spiritual Warrior's Prayer Guide*, Regal Books (2010).

Quin Sherrer, Ruthanne Garlock, *You Can Break That Habit and Be Free*, Chosen Books (2012).

Quin Sherrer, Ruthanne Garlock, *Lord, I Need to Pray with Power*, Charisma (2007).

Quin Sherrer, Ruthanne Garlock, *Lord, I Need Your Healing Power*, Charisma (2006).

Carol Staudacher, *A Time to Grieve*, Harper Collins Publishers (1994).

About the Author

Quin Sherrer has authored or co-authored twenty-nine books, including the best-sellers *A Woman's Guide to Spiritual Warfare*, *Miracles Happen When You Pray*, and *How to Pray for Your Children*. Quin's book, co-authored with Ruthanne Garlock, *God Be With Us: A Daily Guide to Praying for Our Nation* was a finalist for the 2002 Gold Medallion Award in the devotional category, awarded by the Evangelical Christian Press Association.

Quin has spoken to audiences in forty-eight U.S. states and twelve nations, encouraging audiences in their walks of faith. She has addressed topics of prayer, hospitality, miracles, and personal renewal as a guest on more than three hundred radio and television programs (including The 700 Club, 100 Huntley Street, Daystar Television Network and the Trinity Broadcasting Network).

With a degree in journalism from Florida State University, Quin spent her early career writing for newspapers and magazines in the Cape Kennedy, Florida, area, where her late husband, LeRoy, was a NASA engineer. A winner of *Guideposts* magazine's writing contest, she also was named Writer of the Year at the Florida Writers in Touch Conference.

Quin served for some years on the Aglow International board of directors as well as on the United States national Aglow board. She often speaks to church groups, weekend seminars, Sunday congregations, professional groups, and on U.S. military bases. She has three children and six grandchildren.

Contact Quin at: www:quinsherrer.com.